HARRY THOMAS'
MEMORY LANE
VOLUME I

RHYL PRESTATYN
VISITOR

A COLLECTION OF HARRY'S PICTURES & STORIES FROM THE
RHYL & PRESTATYN VISITOR NEWSPAPER COLUMN, MEMORY LANE

Acknowledgements

I am eternally grateful to the following for their more than generous contributions while compiling this book. The very pleasant staff at Gwasg Helygain Ltd, Michael Lewis-Jones, Fred Hobbs, Vivien Hughes-Davies, Jerry Vernon, Pat Jones, Brian Mival and special thanks to Mark Jones, production editor for the Visitor Newspapers for giving me the opportunity to indulge in one of my great passions - local history, and to share it with the readers of The Visitor. Guto Lloyd-Davies, Director of Gwasg Helygain Limited, for his invaluable and ceaseless support in the publishing of this book.

This book is dedicated to those most important in my life: Harry Thomas Junior, Emma Thomas, Jayne McGibbon, Alana May, Mark Tyldesley, may the sky always be painted blue for you. A special mention also to Hazel and Jenny Walker.

In memory of my mother Kath - out of the darkness came a guiding light.

Harry Thomas

November 2003

ISBN: 0 9522755 6 2

by Gwasg Helygain Ltd
68/70 Kinmel Street, Rhyl, Denbighshire LL18 1AW
Tel: 01745 331411 Fax: 01745 331310

Introduction

Since I began writing the Memory Lane column for the Rhyl and Prestatyn Visitor Newspaper in October 2002, I have attempted to pass on some of the immense pleasure, knowledge, interest and passion I have obtained over the years through my extensive archive of old picture postcards and photographs of the locality. I have also endeavoured to chronicle the wealth of rich, colourful, varied stories and historic events connected to Rhyl, Prestatyn and the neighbourhoods past. At the same time exploring the changing images that have left communities and their future generations legacies that shaped their future, made that more clearer and bringing the past into glorious black and white with the benefit of old picture postcards and photographs which are frozen fragments of time giving us a window in which we can all view the past. Showing us a world lost forever.

Many of these legacies from the past were all well-loved crowd pulling attractions and landmarks that local men worked hard taking years to build and left us to savour and enjoy their illustrious achievements. Today these legacies are long gone - demolished without a second thought by those blinkered, tunnel visioned and faceless individuals in an attempt to shape our future.

Yes they are all in this book, landmarks that were Rhyl's Pavilion Theatre, Floral Hall and outdoor swimming pool. Prestatyn's Ffrith, Tower Beach camp and Scala cinema. The passage of time has, without doubt, dealt a very cruel blow to our cherished amenities. We are thankful that memories can't be demolished!

In this book you will also find the Beatles magical history tour on their very first visit to Wales playing in a small club above Burton's the tailors in High Street, Rhyl and later at Prestatyn's Royal Lido. Also featured are Point of Ayr Colliery and the Ironworks at Mostyn, notable industries that stood for over a hundred years employing generations in the community. And just as important was the old Well in Newmarket supplying fresh water to the village for many years, sadly today it is a hole in the ground covered by a rusty metal grating. At a small cost it could be restored to its former glory and turned into an historic feature a lasting memory and tourist attraction for the village.

The corner shop in Rhyl fondly known as 'Aunty Darli's' is also treasuredly remembered as are local figures Emlyn Williams and David Lloyd. Rhyl's mummy in the cupboard and the Ruth Ellis story also feature.

This book was partly written through many comments said to me, and those comments were 'Harry I look forward to reading your Memory Lane column each week, I only wish I had I cut them all out to keep'

Each and every one of us has a yearning for the past and the love of things that are no longer with us, in these days we fall easily into nostalgic mood. It seems we enjoy embracing and thinking more about the past than the present or the uncertain and insecure journey into the unknown we call the future!

There are certain fascinating links to our history and heritage down every street, road, lane and avenue with the most important and valuable lane of all: Memory Lane. I hope you all enjoy the journey!

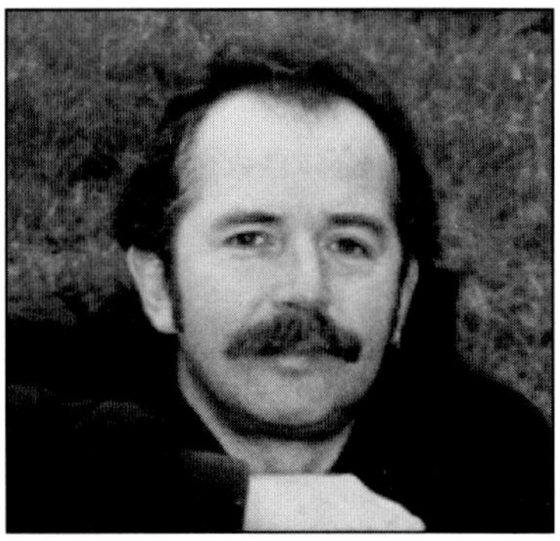

Harry Thomas
November 2003

I am always interested in seeing & copying old photos & picture postcards. If you have any items of local interest please telephone 01745 - 889773.

Foreword

RHYL PRESTATYN VISITOR

For almost ten years I have written, compiled, edited, sub-edited, designed or sub-contracted the Visitor's popular Memory Lane column.

During that time, one name has continually bubbled up to the surface whenever facts needed to be checked or pictures needed to be loaned concerning the good, bad and downright ugly elements of our rich and varied history. That name is Harry Thomas and it is with the greatest of delight that I write the foreword to this, his latest book.

Based on his writings for my paper's Memory Lane column, Harry has put together another tome which not only brings back happy memories for so many people but also chronicles our history and provides those still to come after us with a permanent record of the way we were.

It is often said that over the last hundred years, the development of the human race has moved forward at a faster pace than at any other time in our 75,000 year evolution. Huge advances have been made in technology, medicine, communication, entertainment, transport, social sciences and just about every other field you care to mention but it is still good to hark back to a time when, although life was maybe a wee bit tougher, it was good to be part of a slower, more sedate world where pressure still existed but not in the stress-fuelled, hyperactive, violent and often painful way in which we know it today. Harry's books are a microcosm of life in Rhyl, Prestatyn and the locale as it was. Every picture records a story worth telling and enlightens us about the way our mums, dads, grans and grand-dads, and further back, great-grandparents went about their daily lives. In an age when hi-tech, computer-generated imagery brings roaring dinosaurs into our living rooms, sees secret agents battling villains in outer space, or puts us in charge of Formula One racing cars or military hardware via games consoles, it is good to take one of Harry's books and hark back to a time when conkers, board games and the Saturday matinee gave us our entertainment.

It is easy to become overly sentimental when dealing with nostalgia, but nostalgia, by its very essence, is sentimental. It is the feeling of warmth and affection you get when looking at a picture that brings back happy memories, or reading of an event you attended as a child, or were told about by older people who were part of something you could only imagine happening. It fires the imagination and clarifies points lost in the foggy bits of our minds.

The need to preserve our past is of paramount importance and Harry's books play a crucial role in documenting our local history in all its forms.

I am pleased and proud to be associated with this latest venture of his.

Mark Jones

Production Editor
Visitor Newspaper Series
November 2003

Four Lads who Shook the World... and Rhyl!

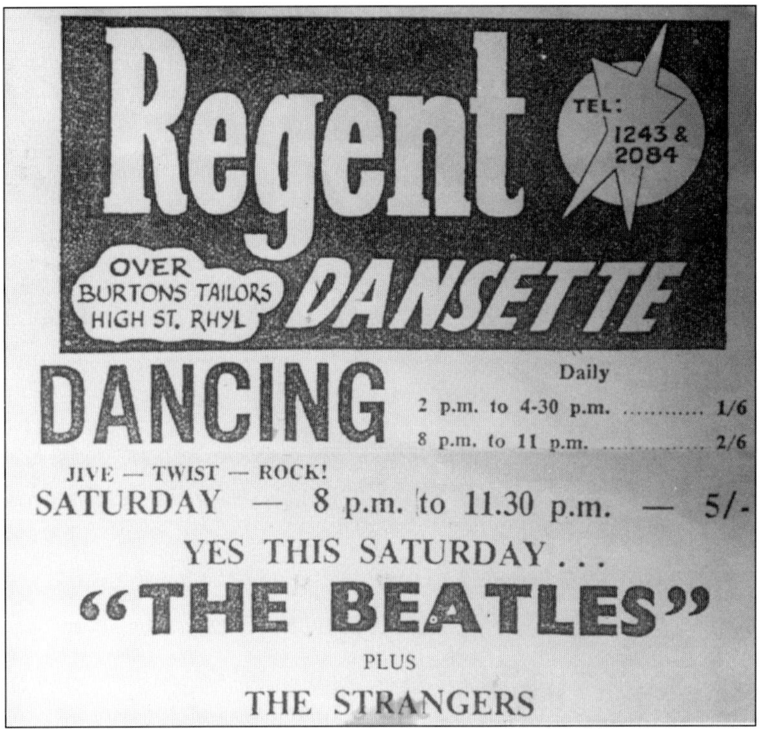

The Beatles first record *Love Me Do* was released on October 5, 1962 and the long and winding road to celebrity status for the Beatles came with the release of their first number one record, *Please Please Me* released in 1963 - the same year that Beatle-mania gripped Britain and later the whole world.

But did the world's most famous pop group ever play in north Wales?

The answer is, yes they did! The first time the Beatles ever played in Wales was at Rhyl on July 14 1962 at the Regent Dansette, a popular club above Burton the Tailor's in the High Street (originally opened in 1945 as a dance studio known as the Regent's Rainbow Room).

The manager of the Regent's Dansette was Joe Young, with his wife helping by supervising the pay box. In one of the rooms at the Regent's was a grand piano and on the night the Beatles arrived, Mrs Young was surprised at hearing John Lennon playing classical music on it as she thought these scruffy, long haired boys dressed in leather jackets and tight fitted trousers were a bunch of yobbos.

Admission to the Regent's Dansette the night the Beatles were playing was five shillings (25p) and it was Pete Best who was playing the drums for them in those days. He was replaced on manager Brian Epstein's orders by Ringo Starr on August 16, 1962.

There was a large stage and dance floor at the Regent and only soft drinks were sold. The popular dances of the day were the twist, the jive and the hippy hippy shake.

The music the Beatles played on the night included *Long Tall Sally, Roll Over Beethoven* and *Money*. John Lennon would always introduce the next song with a witty remark with the rest of the group joining in.

At the end of a very memorable night Pat Jones and her friends from Rhyl asked the Regents manager if they could have the Beatles' autographs and he told them to knock on their dressing room door.

When they did, the Beatles answered the door half naked and dressed only in red underpants. Pat, an innocent seventeen year old, told them that it was

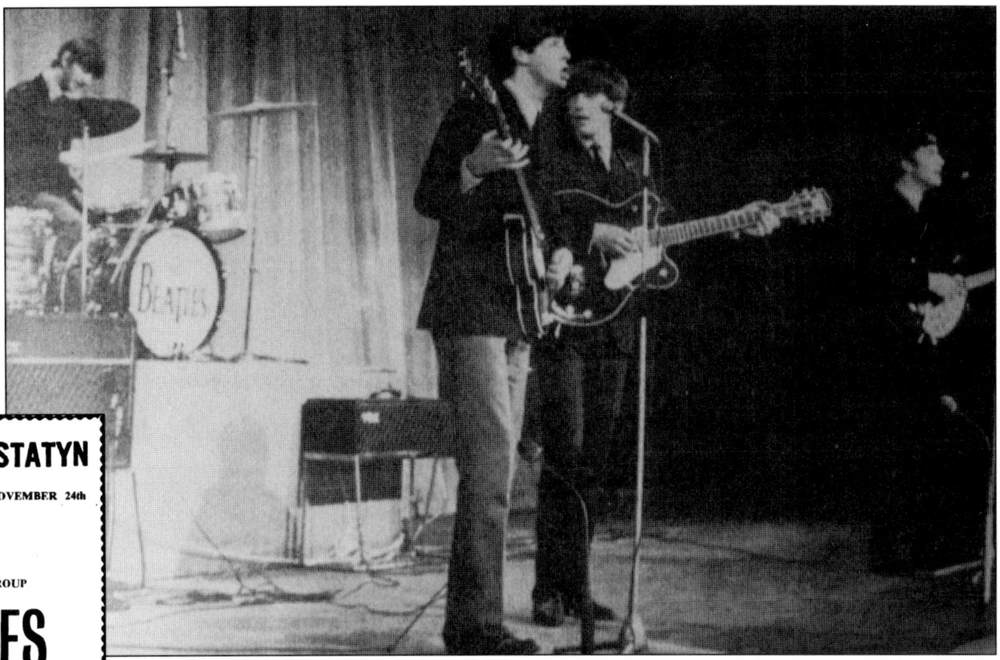

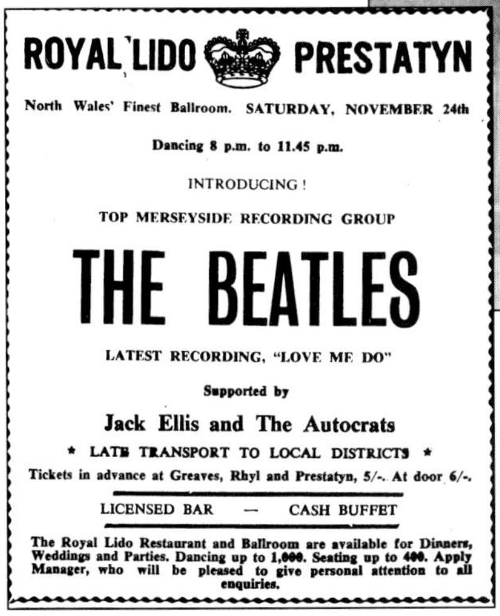

ROYAL LIDO PRESTATYN

North Wales' Finest Ballroom. SATURDAY, NOVEMBER 24th

Dancing 8 p.m. to 11.45 p.m.

INTRODUCING!

TOP MERSEYSIDE RECORDING GROUP

THE BEATLES

LATEST RECORDING, "LOVE ME DO"

Supported by

Jack Ellis and The Autocrats

★ LATE TRANSPORT TO LOCAL DISTRICTS ★

Tickets in advance at Greaves, Rhyl and Prestatyn, 5/-. At door 6/-.

LICENSED BAR — CASH BUFFET

The Royal Lido Restaurant and Ballroom are available for Dinners, Weddings and Parties. Dancing up to 1,000. Seating up to 400. Apply Manager, who will be pleased to give personal attention to all enquiries.

the first time she had seen a man half naked, let alone the Beatles. They all had a joke together and she remembers that the were very much like "the boys next door".

After being given their autographs, Pat and her friends left knowing that they had experienced a lifetime of memories from that night at the Regent.

For that night's performance the Beatles were paid the princely sum of £4. The supporting group to the Beatles were local band the Strangers.

The Beatles' next venue in north Wales was at the Royal Lido, Prestatyn (now the Nova Centre) on November 24, 1962. For their two hour performance at the Lido they were paid £30.

On July 19 and 20, 1963 the Beatles returned again to Rhyl this time playing at the popular Ritz Ballroom (once located where the Ocean Beach Fun Fair is today, destroyed by fire in 1968). The last time the Beatles played in north Wales was at the Odeon Cinema, Llandudno where they played for six nights from August, 1963.

By 1963 the Beatles were established as the world's greatest pop group, at the time each receiving £200 a week from their manager Brian Epstein. At their peak they appeared at the Royal Variety Show in October 1963 when John Lennon infamously remarked *"for those of you in the cheap seats, clap your hands and those of you the expensive seats, rattle your jewellery."* For those of you who were fortunate to see the Beatles play in North Wales you certainly have very treasured memories of four lads who not only shook the world but also shook many clubs here in north Wales. The Beatles disbanded in 1970.

Above: The Beatles on stage at the Royal Lido, Prestatyn November 24th 1962

How Rhyl Played a Part in Screen Lore

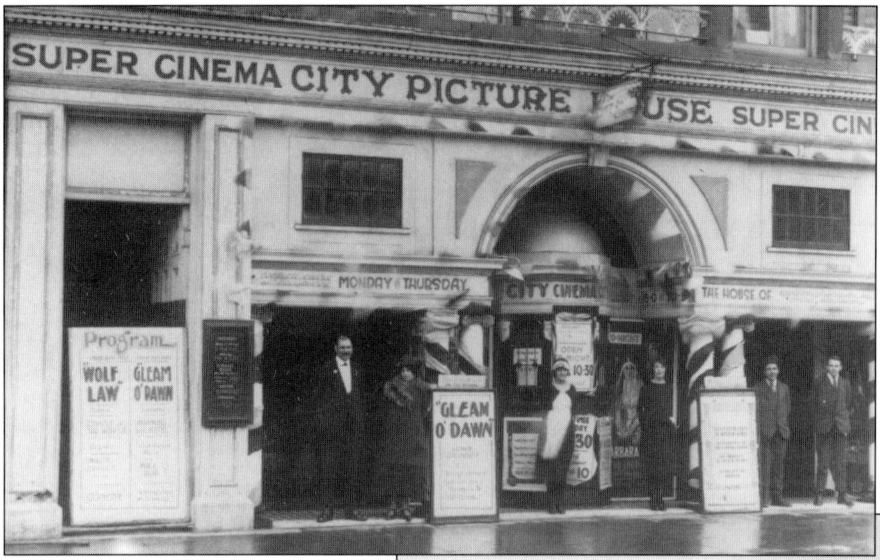

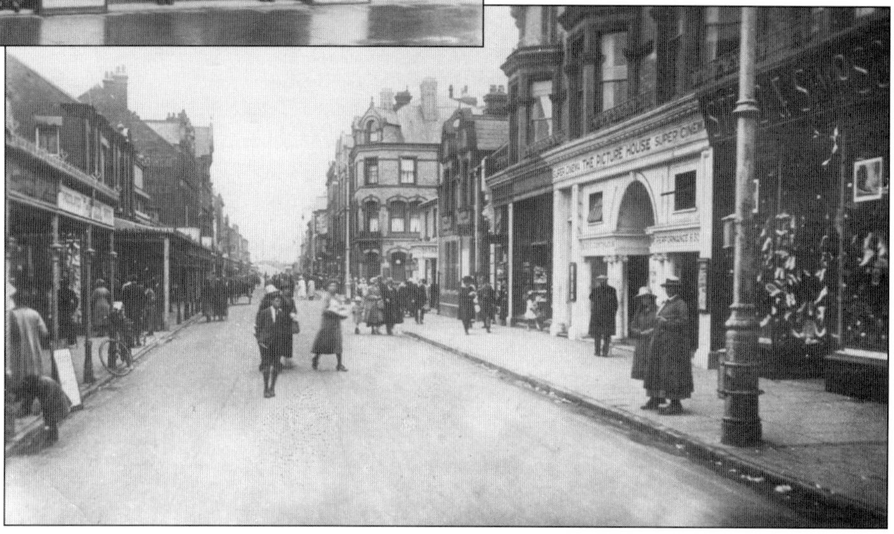

Our bottom picture shows a 1921 scene of a quieter and less hurried looking Rhyl High Street looking towards Vale Road bridge from where Woolworths stands today. In a time when the word stress hadn't entered the English vocabulary, the white fronted building on the right was the very popular Picturedrome cinema and opened in 1911 when films were silent. It was here that some of the first Charlie Chaplin films were screened and music to the films was supplied by a pianist.

The Picturedrome was also known as Kirk's, after its owner, Henry Kirk. In 1921 it changed hands and became known as the City Picture House which introduced the serving of cups of tea at matinee performances before the sale of ice cream at cinemas became commonplace. The City Picture House closed in 1921. Today McDonalds is located here. The attractive and colourful history of Rhyl's cinemas dates back to 1898 and would make a fascinating book in its own right.

There is firm evidenced that the term 'silver screen' originated in Rhyl when the town's famed cinematographer Arthur Cheetham invented the idea of creating brighter, more focused pictures by painting the screen silver at his cinema in Market Street, the Silvograph, opened in 1906 and said to be the very first established cinema in Wales. It later changed its name to the Central Cinema.

Top Picture: Entrance to The Picture House Cinema 1921.

Bottom picture: The white fronted building on the right was the very popular Picturedrome Cinema opened in 1911.

Lazy Summer Days on the High Street

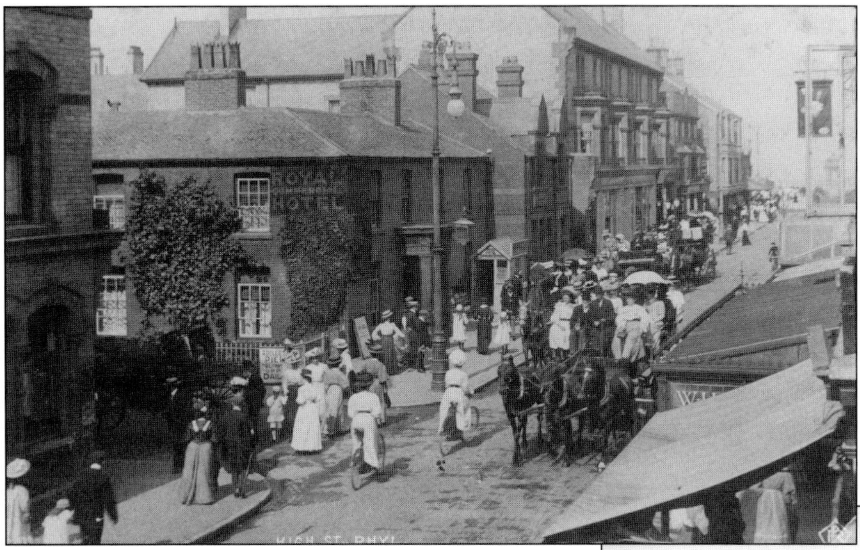

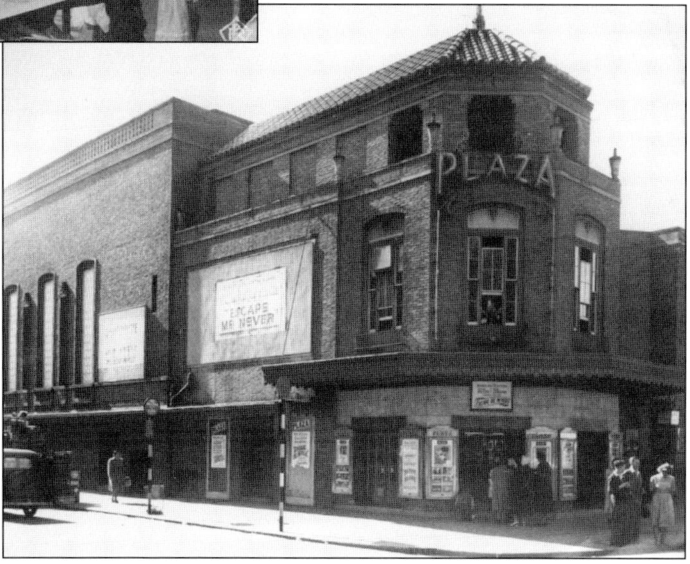

The top postcard features a superb Edwardian study in social history which shows Rhyl High Street in the summer of 1910 when the town was in the height of its popularity as a holiday destination and the pier, Pavilion and Marine Lake attracted thousands of visitors from the large industrial towns and cities of the North and the Midlands.

This postcard also captures a long-gone era once familiar and comforting when a trip to the seaside was an annual event and ginger beer and dandelion and burdock were the great thirst-quenchers during these long, hot summers.

This view shows the Royal Hotel with Sussex Street on the left. When the Royal Hotel was demolished the Plaza Cinema (pictured here in 1947), was built on the site in 1931 and loomed over upper High Street until it was closed in 1986. Today the Piazza restaurant stands on the site of the old Plaza Cinema.

The coach and horses with the ladies holding parasols seen here in Rhyl High Street in 1910, visited local beauty spots which at the time included Bodelwyddan Church, Rhuddlan Castle and Dyserth Waterfalls. The booking office for these tours can be seen near to the Royal Hotel.

Charm and Change in the High Street

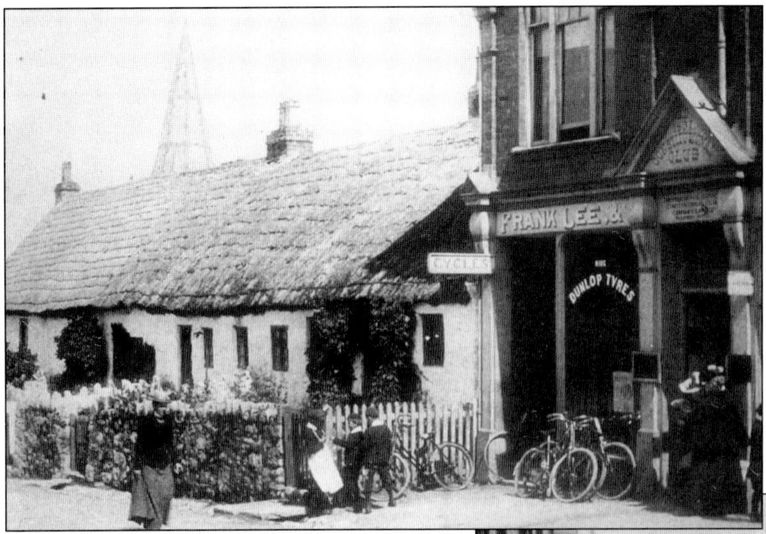

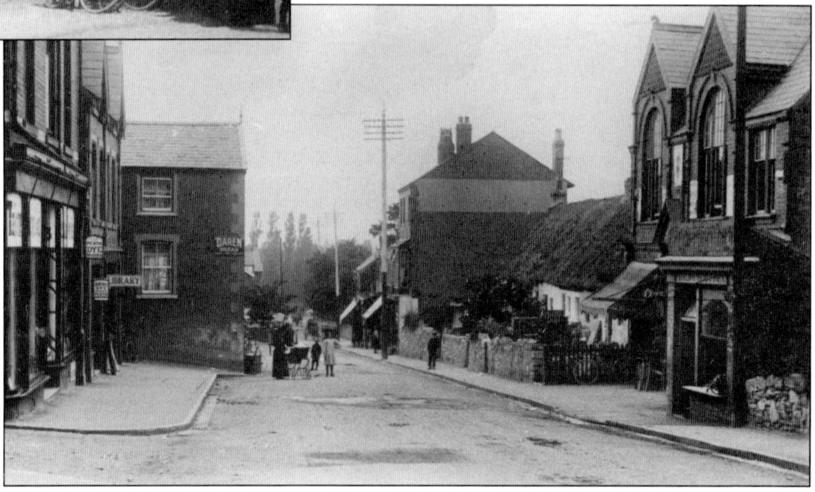

The timeless charm of old Prestatyn is vividly captured on these two picture postcards depicting the top of the High Street in 1910. The building on the right built in 1897 has had a very colourful past and is today the popular Archie's restaurant and bar.

During the 1800's the rooms upstairs here were used as a meeting place for the Liberal Party and also as a games room for playing billiards.

Fred Hobbs of Clwyd Avenue in Prestatyn remembers that during the late 1920's, this building was used by the Salvation Army who offered hot drinks, food and comforting words to the poor of the town. As a nine year old boy Fred remembers having cocoa and toast there!

By the 1930's, the old Liberal rooms had been converted into what was to become the Flintshire County Library and throughout the Second World War the library was widely used by soldiers billeted in the town.

The thatched roofed cottages were an illustrious feature through both sides of the High Street and their photographs appeared on advertisements above the seats in LNWR train compartments promoting the town as an attractive place to visit for a holiday and describing the cottages as "Prestatyn's romantic houses". Eventually, and rather sadly, they became unfit to live in, fell into disrepair and were condemned and demolished.

Seafront Magnets that Drew Millions to Rhyl

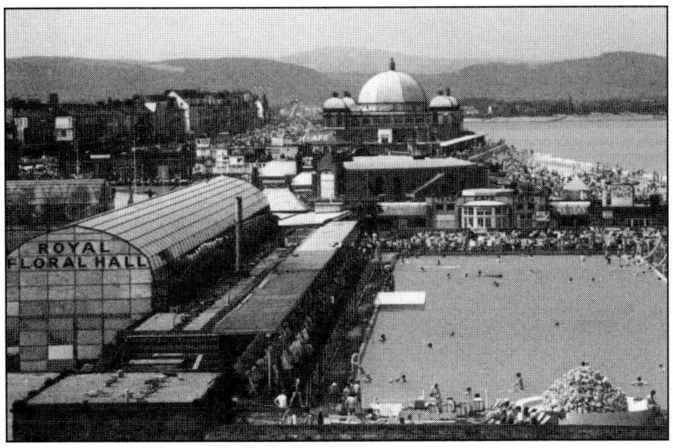

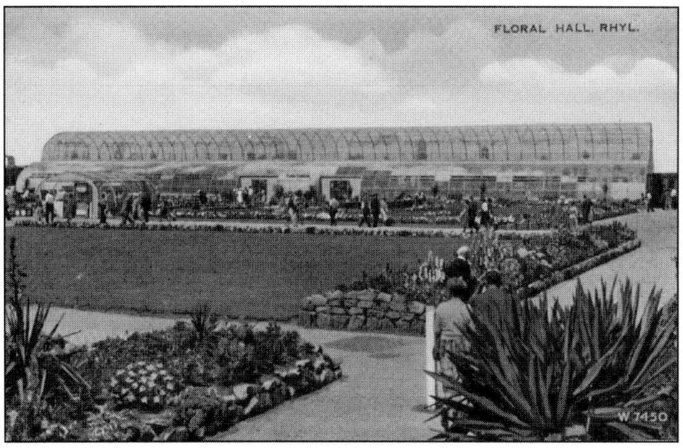

The fondly remembered and well-loved crowd pulling attractions pictured here in the 1970's were landmarks that made Rhyl a mecca for millions of holiday makers over the years and were great legacies to the town from the men of Rhyl who worked hard to build them. How saddened they would be to discover their outcome.

The Floral Hall was built at a cost of £21,000 and opened in 1959 by Roy Turner, Chairman of the Rhyl Urban District Council. During its first three years of opening it was visited by more than a million people including visitors from all over the world who witnessed the floral beauty of it's exotic plants, flowers and cacti; which earned the building the title of *"eighth wonder of Wales."*

After the visit of the Duke and Duchess of Gloucester in 1960 the building was given Royal status and was known thereafter as the Royal Floral Hall. A guide book to the Floral Hall remarked *"where in the world will such beauty be found so close to the sea in the centre of the promenade. Inside you will find a near miracle display of exotic plants, flowers and cacti from countries far away in a blaze of colour, you will also find tropical and foreign birds and butterflies as they all enjoy conditions of free flight"*.

By the late 1980's the Floral Hall had fallen on hard times, plants suffered neglect and vandals had repeatedly broken the glass that made up the building and running costs eventually brought it's downfall. Today the Sea Life Centre is located where the extraordinary Floral Hall once stood.

The open air swimming pool was opened in 1930 by Chairman of the Council J.E. Buckley and was a spectacular amenity offering a 110 yard-long pool that held 775,000 gallons of filtered sea water with decorative bubbling rock fountains at either end of the pool. For those who couldn't swim it was a perennial joy on a hot summer's day to paddle in the shallow end or watch those who displayed their swimming and diving skills as everyday onlookers would pack the 2,500 seats surrounding the pool. It soon became identified as the first pool of its size in Wales to hold recognised swimming competitions and bathing beauty contests. This very popular pool closed in the late 1970's.

Once located where the Skytower is today and seating 1,153 was the 120 foot stately domed Pavilion Theatre opened by Lord Mostyn in 1908. Over the years it held capacity filled summer shows featuring famous entertainers of the day. They included Gracie Fields, Vera Lynn, Arthur Askey, Tommy Trinder, Joe Loss and his Orchestra, Jimmy Jewel and Ben Warris, Mike and Bernie Winters, Harry Seacombe and Shirley Bassey. One of the last summer shows at the Pavilion starred Morcambe and Wise.

The Pavilion was pulled down in 1974 according to the local authority due to cracks in the dome, yet when it was demolished the dome came down in one piece and still intact!

Left Picture: Three crowd-pulling landmarks that made Rhyl a mecca for holidaymakers!

Right Picture: The Floral Hall in its heyday.

Airships, Fair Days and Stocks for the Drunkards

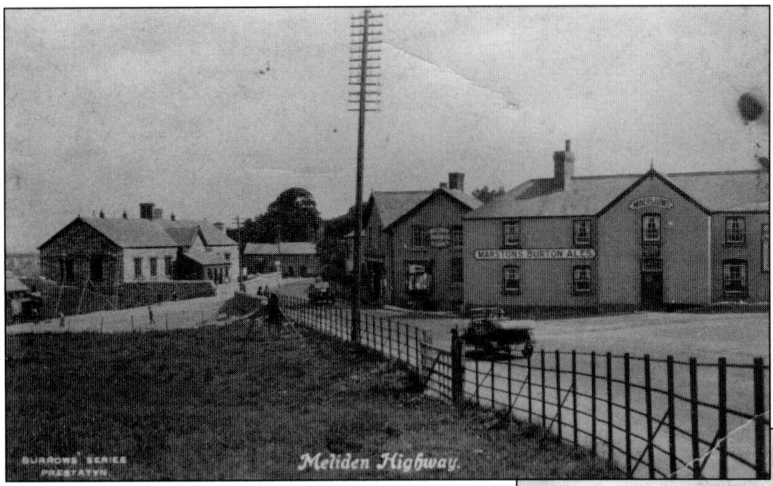

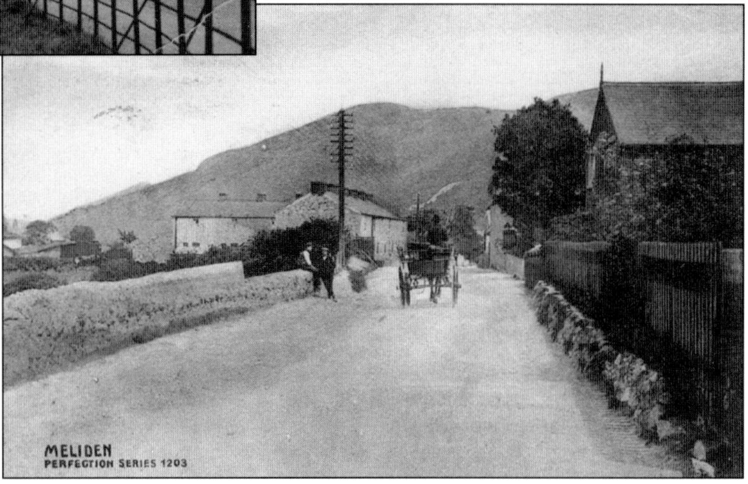

Our bottom picture shows the main road through Meliden in 1909. Mount Pleasant and the miners' cottages on the left are still standing today. Heavy traffic now thunders through here yet the horse and carriage in this picture seems to have an eternity to reach its destination.

Meliden still retains strong links with its history-steeped past through its great sense of community and its stone-built miner's cottages, evidence of a once-thriving lead mining industry. In 1915, when nine-year old Jim Heany (along with the entire village) saw a silver-coloured airship pass over Meliden, he recalls that it had "a red undercarriage which I could clearly see a few thousand feet up in the air". "The only sound coming from it was a low hum. My next door neighbour said to me with a smile; "you watch it doesn't drop any bombs Jim!" The airship eventually moved along the coast towards Llandudno.

The top 1925 postcard shows the Post Office, National School and the Miners Arms (now the Melyd Arms) pub. During the middle of the 1800's on lead miner's monthly paydays, the very popular Meliden fair would be held. Stalls would be set up from the Miners Arms to the Star Inn selling everything from home-baked bread and cakes to home-made sweets, medicines and cure-alls.

Other tempting offers would be Vale of Clwyd mint cake, Meliden rock and a popular ointment known as 'Eli Treffynnon' (Holywell ointment), which claimed to cure gout, ulcers and sore heads. The miners' brass band would complement the day with their music. There were also stocks near the Red Lion for those who drank too much (not a bad idea for some places today!). The Meliden Fair discontinued when the mines closed due to a huge fall in the price of lead in 1883. The population of Meliden in 1871 was 627, today it is 1,800.

Dyserth

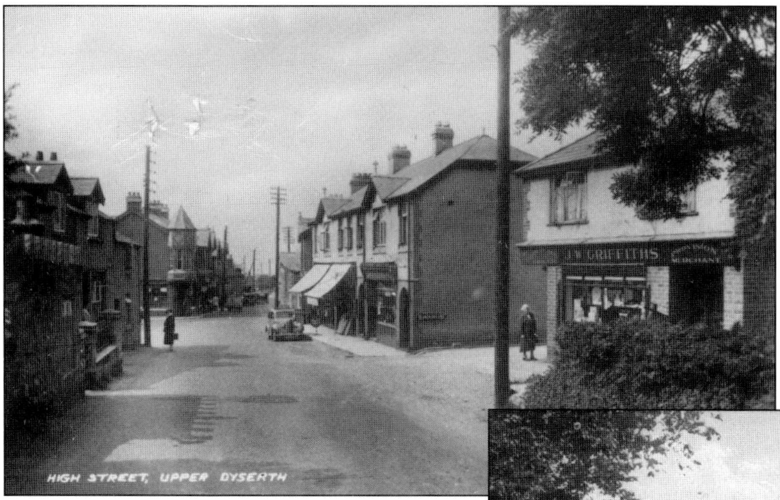

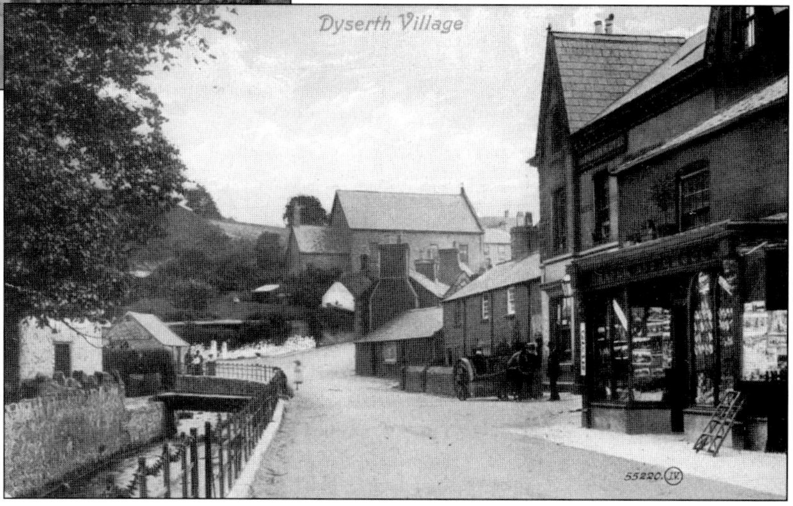

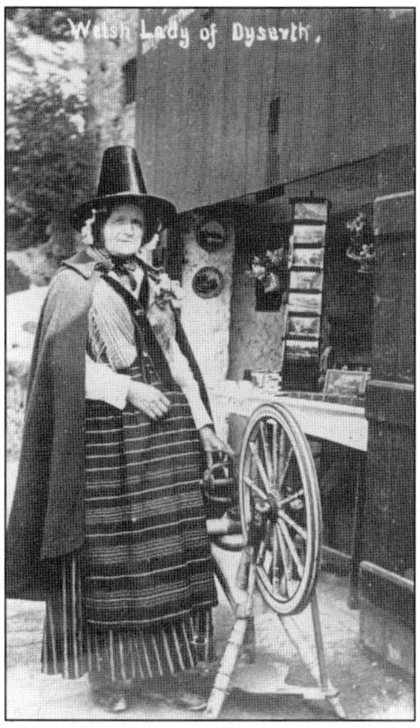

The top postcard is of upper Dyserth in the summer of 1941 J.W. Griffiths grocers and provisions merchant on the right is occupied today by Way Ahead Hairdressers. A guide book of the day says of Dyserth: "The village of Dyserth is fast becoming a popular resort for those seeking rest and quiet, those suffering nervous disorders find the balance of sea and mountain air most beneficial." The earliest record of Dyserth is found in the Doomsday Book of 1086 with the name spelt as Dissard. Dyserth at one time also possessed a famous castle with a rebellious history. Built mainly from local stone by Henry III in 1241 it was razed to the ground by Llewelyn ap Gruffydd's troops in a five week siege in 1263. (A picture of the remains of the castle appears on page 53).

The bottom postcard is of lower Dyserth in 1909, Rob Hughes drapers and grocers on the right was the main grocers shop in this part of the village in those early years and sold everything from dairy produce to clothing, groceries and picture postcards of the village similar to the one seen here. Today part of the Red Lion pub occupies the site of this old shop. The 60 foot waterfalls to the left have been a major North Wales tourist attractions since the early days of the 18th century. Maggie Owen of Dyserth (pictured above) at one time would be dressed in traditional Welsh costume outside the waterfalls cabin shop selling souvenirs and picture postcards to the visitors. One resourceful woman sold waterfall water at one penny (½p) a glass claiming it had curative properties.

A Nostalgic Slice of Life in a Rural Idyll...

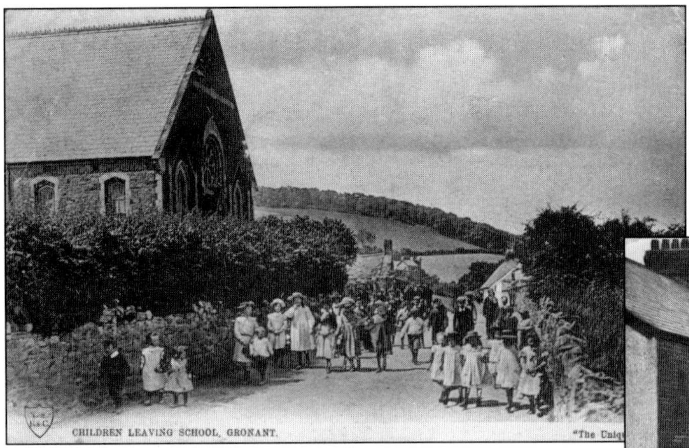

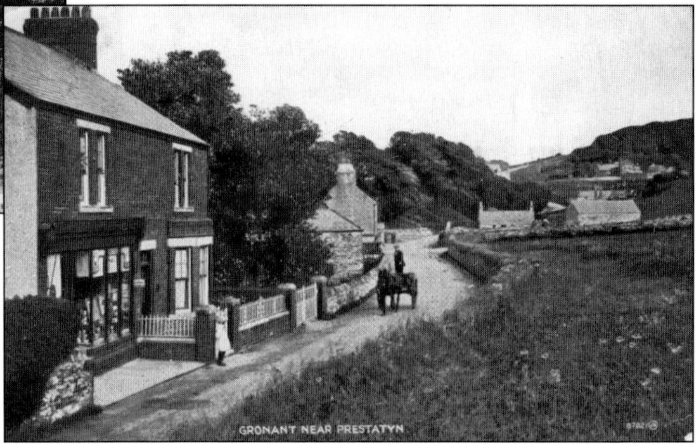

This superbly evocative 1905 postcard shows the children of Gronant posing for a photograph in Llanasa Road after leaving Sunday School. The chapel on the left was the Calvinistic Methodist chapel built in 1870 and demolished in 1991: Llys Capel houses are located here today.

In those days many parents sent their children to Sunday School for a bit of peace and quiet as much as anything, walks in the park and visits to relatives took up the rest of Sunday for children in those days. The wall and field on the right is where Bryn Mor OAP bungalows are today. This is one of my favourite postcards as it is a rich piece of social history frozen in a fragment of time.

Incidentally, did you know that in 1989, a holidaymaker found an unexploded landmine on Gronant Beach? The man carried it to Presthaven Sands where he was staying and when security officers at the camp realised what he had found they put it in a safe place until the bomb disposal team arrived and detonated the mine safely.

On the right is a slumbersome looking Gronant in the summer of 1931. The Gronant Inn is on the far left and dates back to the early 18th century when it was known as the Gronant Arms. Freelands stores on the left was the busiest shop in the village. Owned by Martha Evans it was built in the early 1900's and was the first brick building in Gronant. The shop was shelved all round with a long counter on which stood brass scales and a marble slab for the butter block which was cut into portions and shaped with wooden paddles. Behind the counter stood large green canisters full of loose tea of different qualities, there were also tins of peaches, crab, and salmon plus loose biscuits and sweet jars filled with glacier mints, caramels and treacle toffee also stood on the food-packed shelves.

Salt-encrusted bacon hung from hooks in the ceiling as did enamel jugs for carrying water from springs and wells, medications to cure all ailments were also on sale including tincture of rhubarb, eucalyptus oil and syrup of figs - all were in great demand.

The girl by the gate is Vivien Hughes-Davies, today the village historian who has recently moved to Abergele. Her incredible knowledge of Gronant is helping to preserve the history and heritage of this quaint village. Today, the house that was previously the shop is still called Freelands.

Mining Village's Rich Seam of Memories

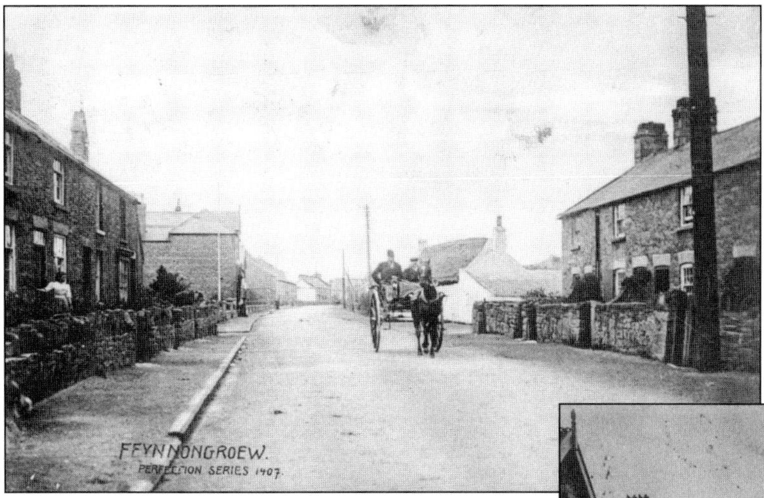

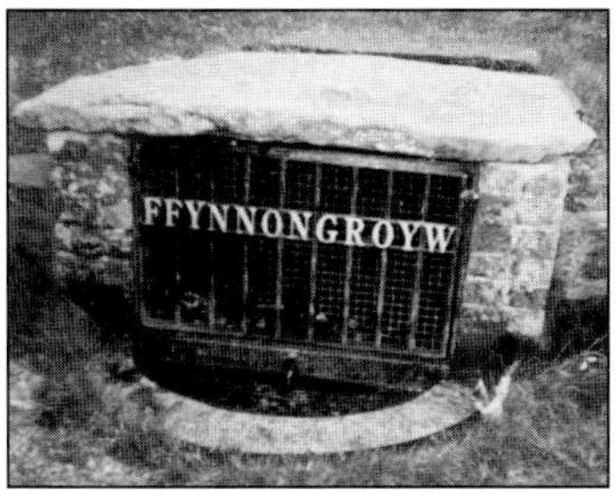

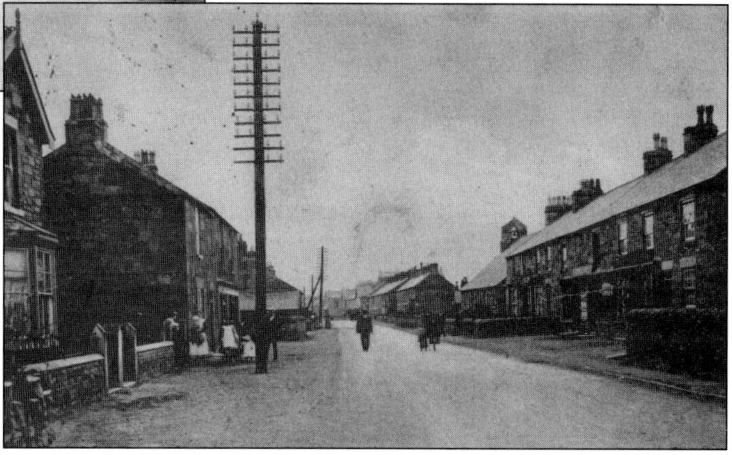

Our top picture shows Ffynnongroyw looking towards Mostyn from the Farmer's Arms in 1908. Uwchlyn Cottages on the right look very similar today as does School Row on the left.

'Twmpath', the whitewashed cottage on the right at the corner of Well Lane is the oldest dwelling in the village. The doors and windows to this building are facing south for protection from high tides at a time before land reclamation when water from the estuary came very close to this building's walls- this was also, at one time, used as a communal bakehouse.

Less hurried and more contented days are depicted in this 1912 postcard (on right) of Ffynnongroyw. This view is looking towards Prestatyn from the Crown Hotel, Kidderminster Cottages are pictured on the right and it was here at Kidderminster House that E H Williams had his shop. He was well-known to the housewives in the village in those days for his top quality pork and bacon. As early as the 1860's shops were plentiful and varied in this small village mining community and included a drapers, grocers, chemist and a butchers.

By 1889 there were three taverns in the village (as there are today) - the Farmers, the Railway and the Crown. Did you know that Ffynnongroyw was at one time famous for its spring well (from where the village name originates). Miners at Point of Ayr Colliery used to fill up their flasks with water at the well and it also supplied the villagers with fresh drinking water for years.

The legend is told that 300 years ago, shipwrecked sailors came ashore at Ffynnongroyw in search of drinking water and discovered a well which they named Clear Crystal Well (Ffynnongroyw). In later years it became unfit to drink and was boarded up in the 1950s. Today this ancient and historic well has been cleared, tidied up and fitted with an ornamental covering and is now quite a tourist attraction which is well worth a visit to see.

Tales of Randy Rabbits and German Spies...

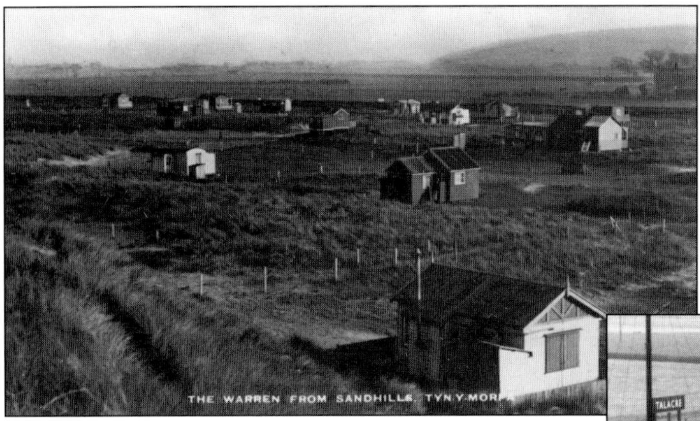

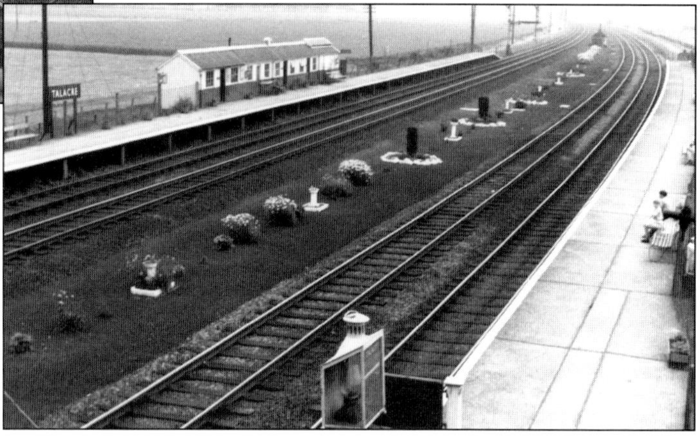

The small yet popular holiday resort of Talacre cannot be talked about without the legendary Warren coming into the conversation. The warren was an area of land between Shore Road, Gronant and Talacre. Its name came about due to the high rabbit population released to breed and populate to provide sport and food for Talacre Hall Estate who owned the land. During the early 1900s, any poachers caught on the land were fined heavily and exiled from the area. In 1920 the Warren was offered for sale along with the rest of Talacre Estate.

It was after this that a large number of unusual dwellings appeared on the site. These curiosities ranged from scrapped double-decker buses to railway carriages and small wooden sheds. During the summer season, little shops and bakeries flourished (no doubt selling rabbit pie!) and in the war years it became full with evacuees, mainly from the Merseyside area.

During the winter these flimsy dwellings were unsafe to live in as candles, paraffin lamps and crude chimneys created fire hazards. Nothing now remains of the old warren and the land has been transformed into a conservation area and popular walkway by its owners, BHP.

On the right is Talacre railway station looking towards Prestatyn in the 1950s. Opened in 1903 it became one of the busiest stations in North Wales throughout the summer months as thousands of holiday makers descended on the station in the 1940s, 50s and 60s to spend their holidays in Talacre's caravans and chalets.

Talacre made headlines in the early 1940s when Davy Hughes, the owner of Talacre Stores on the Coast Road, was crossing the railway bridge to deliver groceries he noticed a suspicious looking car with two men inside who had been loitering around for a few days. He called the police and they kept watch and eventually followed them to a bungalow on the warren where they lived.

When the police raided the bungalow they found it full of radio equipment and later discovered they were German spies who had been taking numbers of goods trains from their car on the railway bridge and relaying the information back to the Fatherland!

Top postcard: The Warren in 1941

A Celebration of our Christmasses Past...

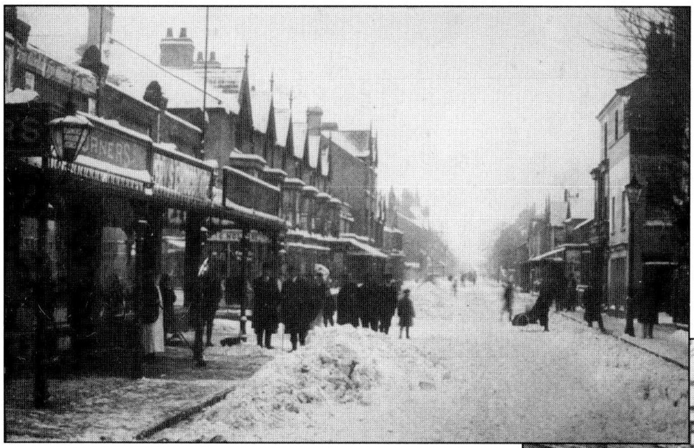

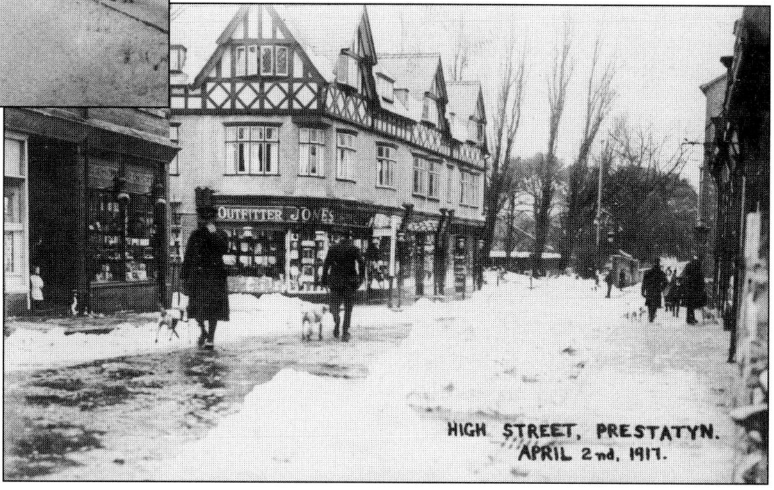

There were many poor people in Rhyl and Prestatyn in the early 1900s as there was no welfare state to help the unemployed. In 1910 a report reveals that: "the members of the Poor Relief Committee met at Rhyl Town Hall on December 23 and distributed a large number of tickets for hot pots and coal for the poor of the town. The hot dishes will be distributed from various bake houses in Rhyl."

We all yearn for a white Christmas (just like the ones we used to know) but in fact, in the last 40 years there have only been five years when we celebrated a white Christmas - the last being in 1976. In the past, Christmas was celebrated in traditional style when compassion and respectability were qualities inbred. Thick blankets of snow on groaning roofs and the images of shop windows dressed to an art were all features of the day.

Butchers shops similar to Espleys in Sussex Street, Rhyl and Dowells at the top of the High Street in Prestatyn displayed suckling pigs, home-made sausages, pork pies and home-bred turkeys, competed with grocers like EB Jones and the Star Supply Stores where eyes feasted on dates and figs in fancy boxes, Christmas cakes crammed to bursting with fruit, fancy biscuits and much more. Festive treats at EB Jones' included 16 mince pies for 1/- (5p), Christmas puds rich in fruit for the same price and jars of mincemeat at a halfpenny. HA Steers wine merchants in High Street Rhyl in the early 1900s sold Bass beer at 2/6d (12 ½p) for a dozen bottles and gallon bottles of whisky for 42/- (£2.10).

The Alexandra Hotel, Rhyl, advertised Christmas dinners in 1910 at 1/-(5p) while Kirk's tobacconist on West Parade, Rhyl, was selling Merrie Men cigarettes at 2/- (10p) for one hundred!

The last word goes to Smally's toy shop poster: "Christmas comes but once a year so give the kids a treat, bring them all to Smally's store down on Bedford Street."

The top postcard is of Wellington Road under snow in 1910, looking towards the Foryd Bridge from where the Police Station is today.

Prestatyn's Ffrith Remembered

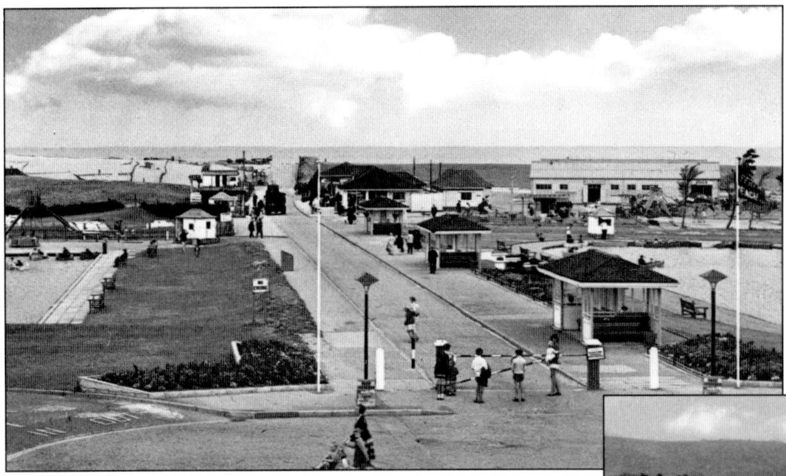

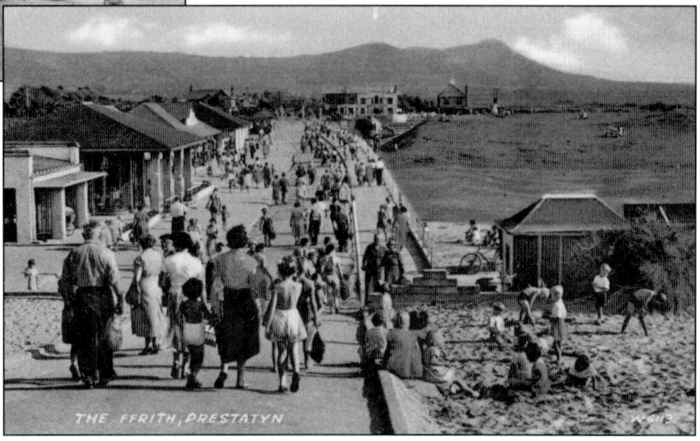

Prestatyn's Festival Gardens, standing on land once occupied by the romantic settings of the Ffrith, is in the news again and up for sale. Let's remind ourselves how valuable an asset the Ffrith was to Prestatyn and what a monumental disaster it was to demolish what was a highly-popular paradise for both holidaymakers and families living in the area.

In 1933, Prestatyn Town Council made arrangements to purchase 75 acres of land for £26,000, later to become known as the Ffrith. Previously, the land formed part of the Pulleyne Estate, part of which were parish allotments and looked very unsightly.

Councillor Eleanor Evans, later to become Prestatyn's first lady mayor, suggested that the developed land should be called "Traeth Gorllewinol" (Western Beach) - but this was considered too difficult to pronounce and eventually Y Ffrith was adopted and opened on August 1, 1935, by Coun G A Plimmer who opened the gates with a silver key while dedicating the area to the public and people of Prestatyn "for all time."

A contemporary guide book for the town describes the Ffrith as: "a very popular bathing and pleasure centre which has become a mecca for thousands of holidaymakers and visitors alike.

"A broad green lawn and valley between the sand dunes is ideal for bathing or for the enjoyment of the lovely views of the hills and the Vale of Clwyd.

"Artistic shelters, a modern café and other amenities flank the drive leading from the main gates of the Coast Road, a model yacht pool is a perennial joy to the young and there is a boating lake, kiddies corner, putting green, crazy golf and indoor skating rink with parking for 1,750 cars.

"Sunshine and colour give the Ffrith a continental air and in the season, a special toast-rack bus from the town is busy all day"

We all have special memories of the Ffrith and thankfully, memories can't be demolished!

The top postcard is dated c1970.

The bottom postcard is of the Ffrith in its heyday in 1958.

Glorious Gwespyr's Heyday

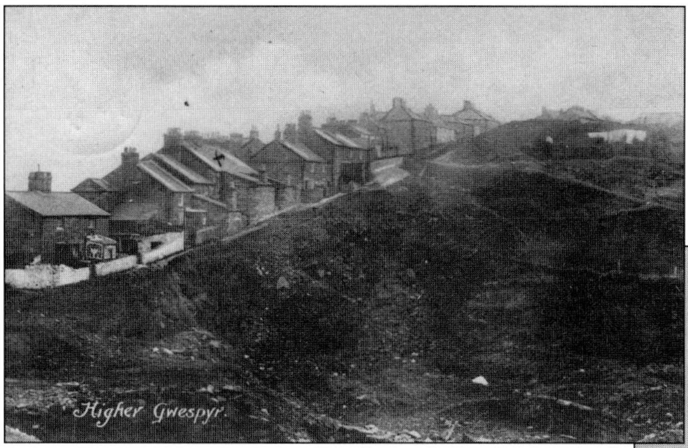

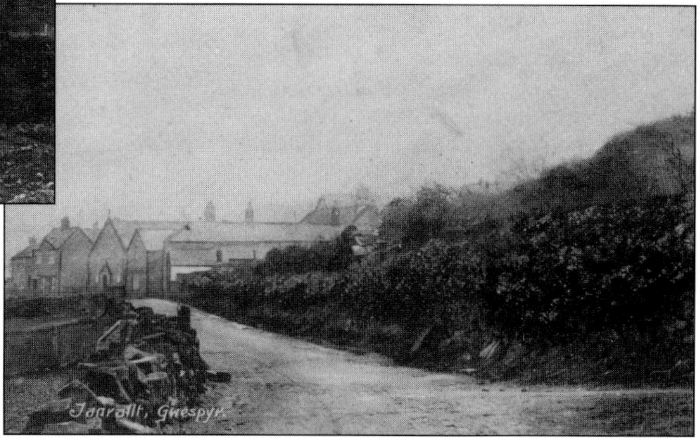

Gwespyr has a neighbourly charm that would rival any village of its size in Wales and the jaw dropping view from Gwespyr of the Dee Estuary and beyond would create a most captivating picture postcard.

The 1922 bottom postcard of Gwespyr is looking towards Dee View cottages and is totally unrecognisable from today's vista of modern houses although some vestiges of old Gwespyr can still be seen.

The top postcard is dated 1921 and shows Llanasa Road with Proffit Terrace on the left, the village Hall, opened in 1951, is today located on the right.

Gwespyr was once known as Wesberie and is of Scandinavian origin. During the eighth and 10th centuries, Viking raiders and traders settled along the North Wales coast and Gwespyr was known as a Viking settlement. Some evidence of this was found in 1931 when a Viking warrior's grave was discovered near to where Lloyd's caravans are situated today in Tan Lan. The discovery of a rusty spearhead in the grave along with rust marks on the six-foot skeleton's spine was the probable result of a spear piercing his body causing his death. The Viking skeleton is kept at the Natural History Museum in London.

Gwespyr was also famed worldwide for its top-quality stone quarried in quantity from Roman times and shipped around the world. "Gwespyr Stone" as it has become known had a fine grain and colour and a remarkable quality of cutting and shaping. It was used in many buildings in and around Gwespyr including the ancient Maen Achwyfan at Whitford, the chapel above St Winifride's Well in Holywell, stone carvings on Rhuddlan and Denbigh castles, St Asaph cathedral, the Talacre Arms pub in Gwespyr and Greenfield's Basingwerk Abbey.

Gwespyr stone was also found at the sites of Prestatyn Castle and the Roman bath-house in Prestatyn.

I have the happiest memories of growing up in Gwespyr and have the fondest love for the village and its people, so let me share one of my recollections with you. Every Sunday during the summer in the 1960s "Arthur Ice Cream" would visit the village and my mother would send me out to him with a bowl and instructions to get six pennyworth of ice cream. It would be the exact same bowl she applied to myself and my brother's heads to cut our hair - without the ice cream in it of course!

How a Growing Village Relied on its Well...

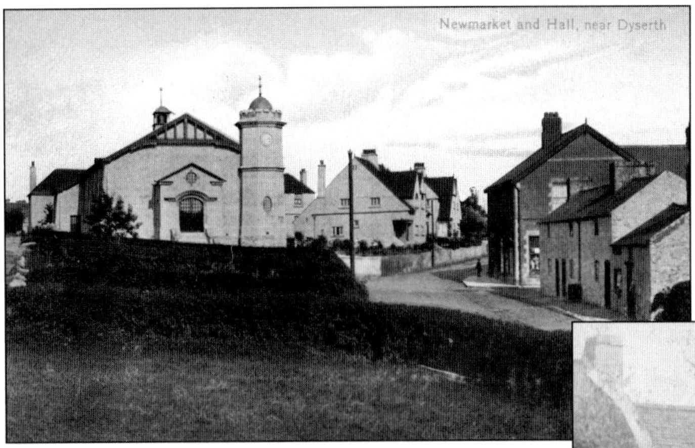

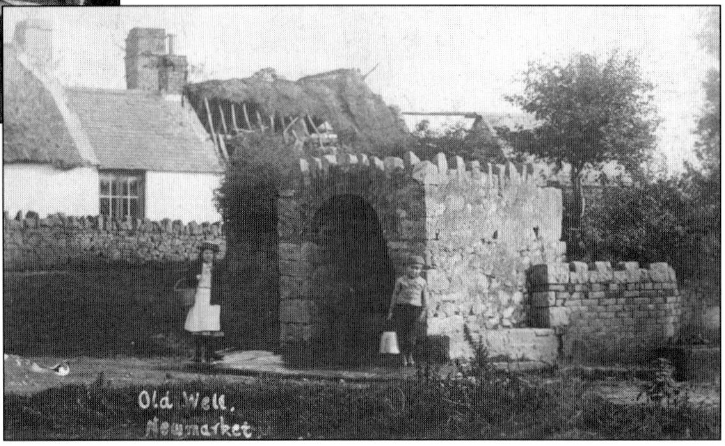

The quaint village of Trelawnyd is first mentioned in the Domesday Book of 1086 as Trevelesnu but over the years, many people unfamiliar with Welsh attempted to pronounce in their own accents and henceforth a variety of names appeared including Trelawnyd, Drelownyd and Relawnid.

To stop this name confusion, John Wynn of Y Gop obtained authority from the Bishop's Registry in St Asaph in 1700 to replace the name of the parish and due to the then recently established annual fair and weekly market in the village, Newmarket was chosen.

The village was officially named Trelawnyd in 1954 and its main feature the Gop, is the second-largest man-made mound in Europe. The purpose of its construction is shrouded in mystery although past excavations disproved it as a burial mound, it was possibly built as an identifiable landmark to guide ancient travellers before roads or tracks were built.

Another main feature of Trelawnyd is the War Memorial Hall built by Michael Anthony of Mia Hall Trelawnyd in memory of his wife Polly Mia! Built at the end of World War One, it has represented an important part of life in the village ever since. It is pictured here (top) c1920.

In the mid-1800s, when the population was 631, Trelawnyd had three tailors, seven grocers, a blacksmith, five shoemakers and three butchers shops all helping in the economy of the then-bustling village life. In the days before water was piped into their homes, the village possessed a spring water well which became the main supply for washing, cooking and drinking.

People were wholly dependent on it, while farmers visited the well to fill large barrels for their cattle. Even during the hottest of summers there was no record of the well running dry. The passage of time has dealt a cruel blow to the well in Well Lane. After faithfully serving the community for years, it is now a hole in the ground covered by a metal grating. Surely at a small cost it could be restored to its former glory and turned into an historic feature and a tourist attraction for the village. The 1910 postcard of the well seen here is a delightfully charming study of the well in full use.

Mining Into a Deep Seam of Our Heritage

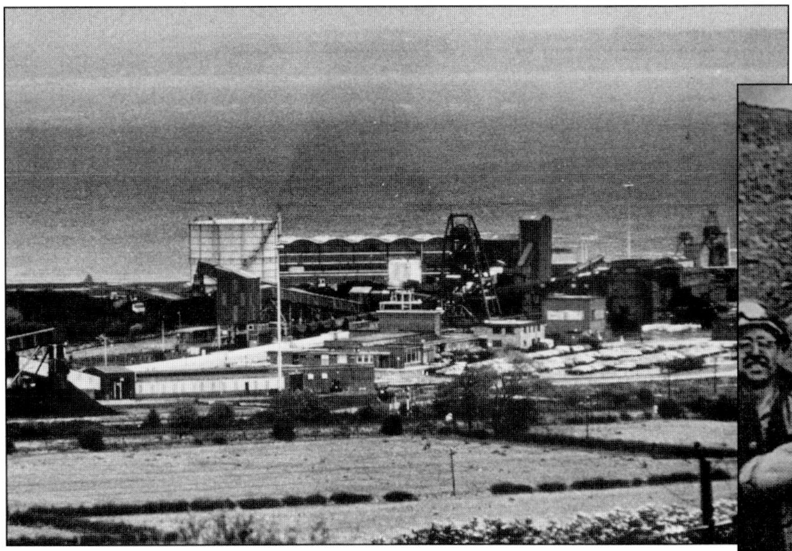

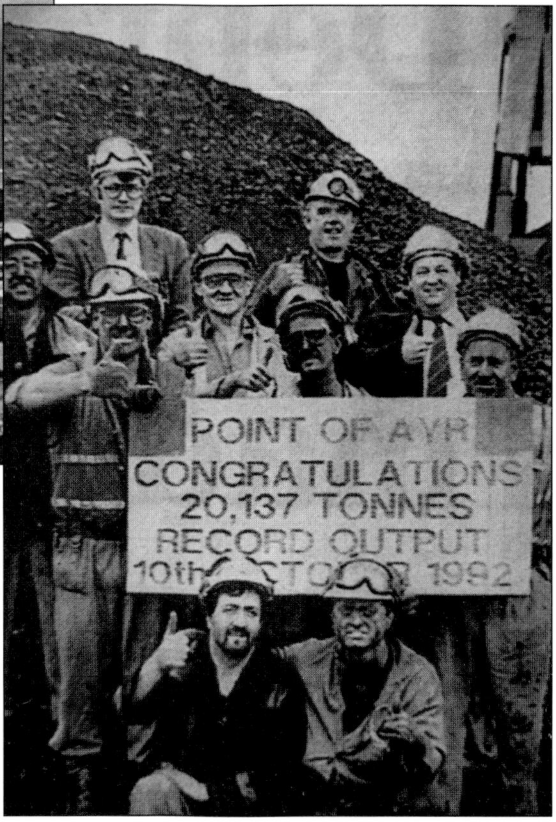

Nothing now exists of the once notable Point of Ayr Colliery (pictured above the year it closed in 1991) and sadly there is no memorial of where it once stood, mining for coal under the Dee Estuary for 133 years. Thankfully, old postcards and photographs are an invaluable source of preserving our history and heritage and capturing long-lost memories.

The communities around Point of Ayr relied either directly or indirectly on the pit for their living and also depended heavily on coal as fuel for their heating and cooking. The first boreholes at Point of Ayr were sunk in 1865 but there were many engineering difficulties to overcome and it was not until the 1880's that the first good quality coal was produced.

The coal at that time was brought to the surface with the help of 75 pit ponies that were used to pull the coal carts. One third of the total output of Point of Ayr was loaded onto boats which plied between the Isle of Man and the West Coast.

In 1984 the miners saw the governments policy to close uneconomic pits as a threat to all their jobs and whole communities became united in a bitter, and sometimes violent national strike. By 1985 nearly 50,000 miners nationally had returned to work without a settlement, while at Point of Ayr 84 miners from a workforce of around 700 stayed out on strike until the bitter end.

The hundred-year old history which Wales had become famous for and where coal was once thought of as "black gold" has now come to an end.

Right photograph: An historic picture for the record books showing Point of Ayr miners in high spirits after achieving a record out-put of 20,000 tonnes of coal in 1992.

In the picture are: Dougie Blair (Assistant Manager), Terry Evans (A.K.A. as Terry Eggs), Mike Morton (A.K.A. Rottweiler), John Lloyd, Ken Lea, Brian Marshall, Philip Cooper, Islwyn Luke (renowned dart player at the Railway Inn, Ffynnongroyw), Terry Hughes (A.K.A. Terry Delicate), Russ Williams

Rhyl High Street, 1885 bc

(that's Before Commercialism)

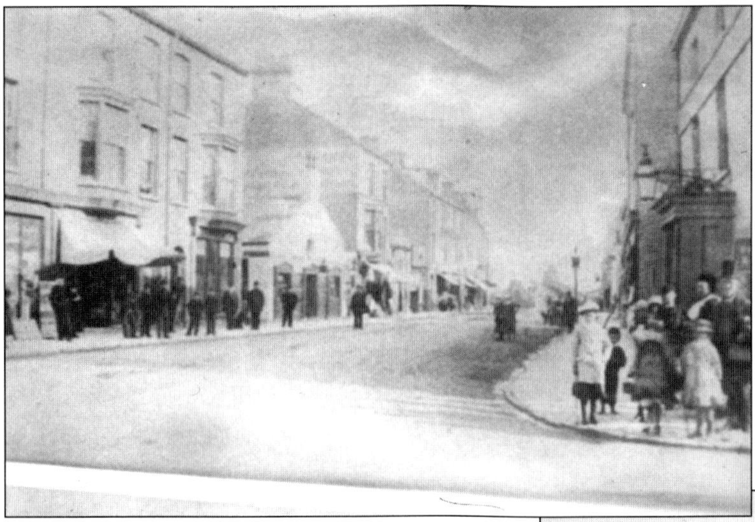

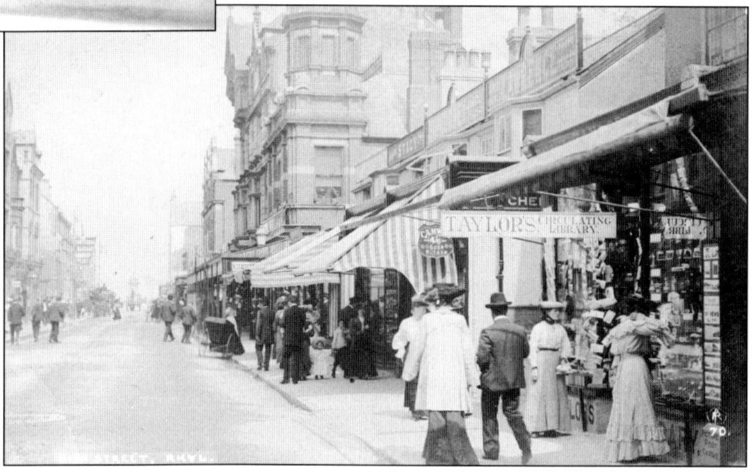

The earliest known photo of Rhyl High Street is seen here (top) in 1885, looking towards the Vale Road bridge - which opened in 1855 - from the corner of Wellington Road.

The white building centre left was the towns police station, the New Inn is sited here today. In 1891 it was sold to Albert Greenall and Co. for the princely sum if £1,025 and in 1976 the pub changed its name to the Kestrel and became a highly-popular and friendly drinking establishment with a famous disco upstairs. This venue, along with the Palace Hotel, provided me with many happy days and some unforgettable nights!

When this photo was taken it was to be another 16 years before electric lighting was introduced to the streets (1901) and another 10 years before Rhyl had its first cinema, the Silvograph in Market Street. The population of Rhyl was then just 6,000 (1999 census 26,489).

The opening of Rhyl railway station in 1848 saw vast numbers visit from larger towns and cities to spend a day out or stay awhile and many fell in love with the area and eventually settled - a new chapter in Rhyl's history had dawned. As the years passed Rhyl grew and prospered, surviving war and unrest and becoming the most popular holiday destination in North Wales in those early years.

The 1907 postcard below is a vividly-captured Edwardian shopping scene and I find the fashion in clothes in those days totally intoxicating - what do you think? This part of the High Street has since been demolished and rebuilt where H. Samuel, Barratt Shoes and Clinton Cards are today sited, between Marks and Spencer and Boots the Chemist.

Treasure Trove of Silver Coins Hidden Up Chimney

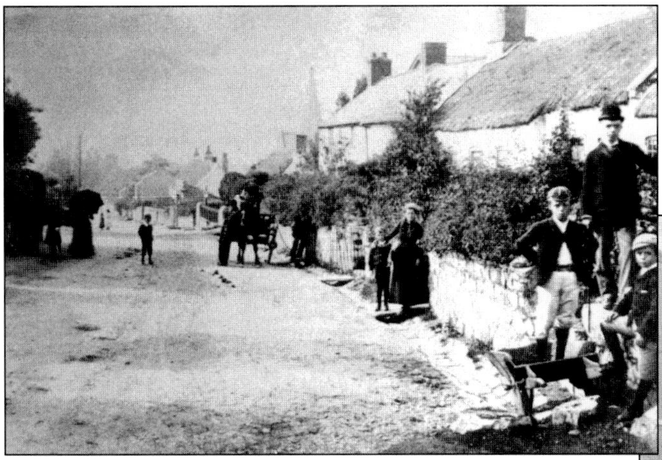

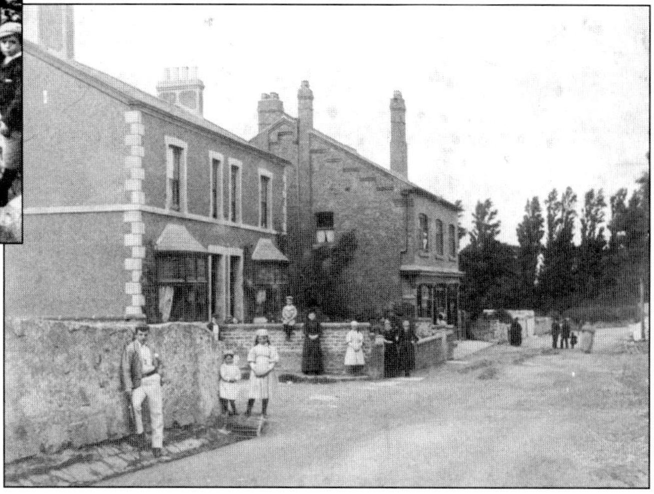

This thought-provoking rural-looking scene (top photo) with its thatched cottages and shrubbery is looking down Prestatyn High Street in 1885 from where Books Unlimited is today. The spire of the parish church, built in 1863, dominates the skyline in a photograph that positively reeks of the past as it captures the tranquil, slumbersome and less hurried days of Prestatyn as a village.

In those days the High Street curved from side-to-side, the road was also unsurfaced and devoid of any footpaths and street lighting - did the phrase "things that go bump in the night" originate in Prestatyn I wonder? An open gutter also ran down one side of the street which most of the time flowed with water that became a fast-running stream when the rain fell. Flagstones bridged the gutter, enabling residents to cross and remnants of this ancient stone guttering can still be seen along Fforddlas.

When the cottage on the right was demolished in 1934 a hoard of 519 silver shillings, sixpences, a half-crown and two groats were discovered in the chimney, dating back to the reigns of Elizabeth I (1558-1603), James I (1603-1625) and Charles I (1625-1649).

An inquest on the hoard was held at Prestatyn's Council Chamber and the coroners judgement was that a former resident of the cottage had hidden the money for safe keeping and it was therefore declared as treasure trove as no-one had come forward to claim it.

When the cottages were demolished and the hoard was discovered it was deposited in a bucket on the footpath nearby and passers-by noticing it took a coin home as a souvenir, being allowed to do this by watching workmen on condition they weren't sold. The British Museum later acquired 113 coins and the National Museum acquired 50 while subsequent research discovered that they were hidden around 1643. Powells the Jewellers and Morrice-Evans Opticians are now located where these cottages once stood.

The captivating middle of High Street photo (bottom) looks down the street in 1885 from where Save with Dave is today (previously Masons the grocers). Victoria Avenue is the road on the left while the building on the left, long since gone, is where Barclays Bank stands today.

How a Rainy Day Read Sparked a Literary Life

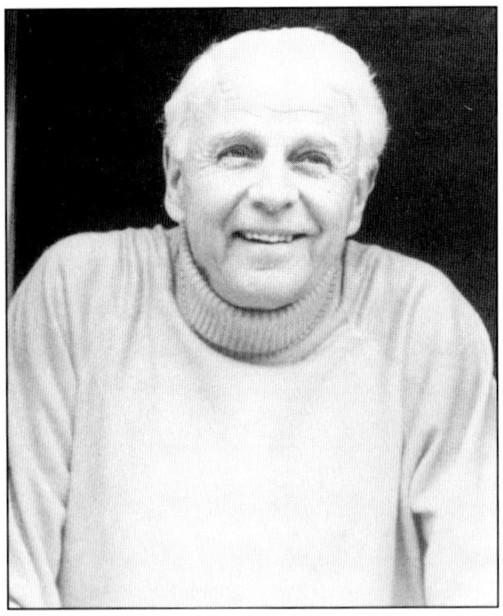

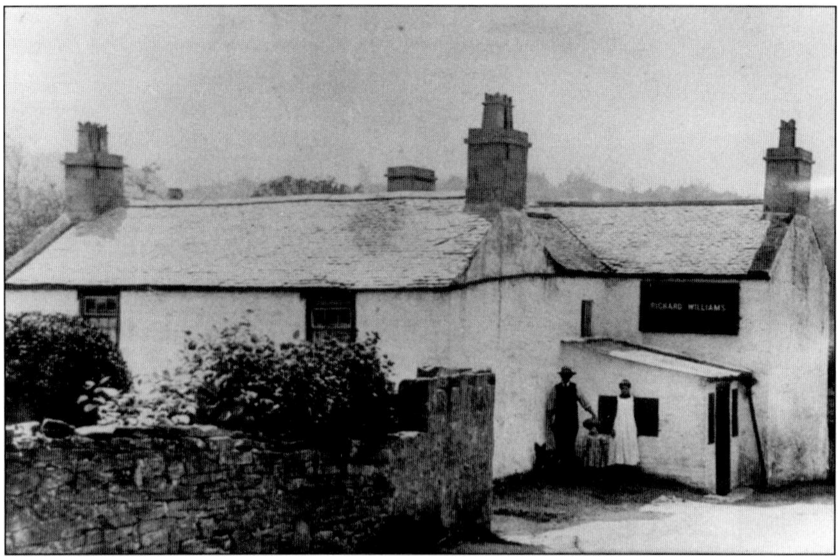

One rainy day in 1912, during the school holidays, six-year-old Emlyn Williams, son of Richard and Mary Williams, asked their home help, Annie Roberts, for something to read. She gave him a battered copy of the novel "The Welsh Singer" and this proved the catalyst that fired Emlyn's blood with the love of words that was later to take him to an Oxford scholarship and international fame as an author, actor and playwright.

Emlyn Williams was born in 1905 at 1, Jones Terrace, Penyffordd (a plaque on the house commemorating his birth can be seen there today). Emlyns parents later moved to the White Lion Inn, Glanyrafon, where they lived for nine years. Emlyn remembers having to walk up to Llanasa to visit the Post Office and down to Ffynnongroyw for everything from a box of matches to a bottle of medicine.

E.B. Jones' van from Prestatyn would call with provisions once a week . At the age of four, he began his education at Talacre School where he first learnt to write in English although it was much later that he actually learnt to speak it.

Emlyn then moved to Picton School when it opened in 1914 being one of the very first pupils there, and a year later his parents gave up the White Lion and moved to number One, Mainstone Cottages in Trelogan where Emlyn attended the council school. He now read avidly and one favourite magazine was the "Old Companion" for which he would walk a mile every Monday to Glanyrafon to buy a copy.

On the way home, reading the "Companion", he would become so engrossed by the weekly serial story that he would often walk into ditches or down the middle of the road with Point of Ayr miners on their way home from work cycling around him and calling out good-humoured insults.

Emlyn eventually took his exams and this is when he first met Sarah Cook who recognised his talent and later helped him to obtain his Oxford scholarship. Sarah was to remain his lifelong friend and was later immortalised as Miss Moffat in "The Corn is Green" (later to become a classic film), his most famous work which he wrote in 1938 about his life in a Welsh mining village. The spark of creativity needed to seek what is best in us and to find the finer things in life is in us all, as Emlyn proved. He died at his London home in 1987.

Left Photo: Emlyn Williams in 1985.

Right Photo: Early beginnings: The White Lion Inn, Glanyrafon c1910. Pictured outside are five-year-old Emlyn Williams, his father Richard and Emlyns aunt.

One of The Greatest Voices Wales has ever Produced

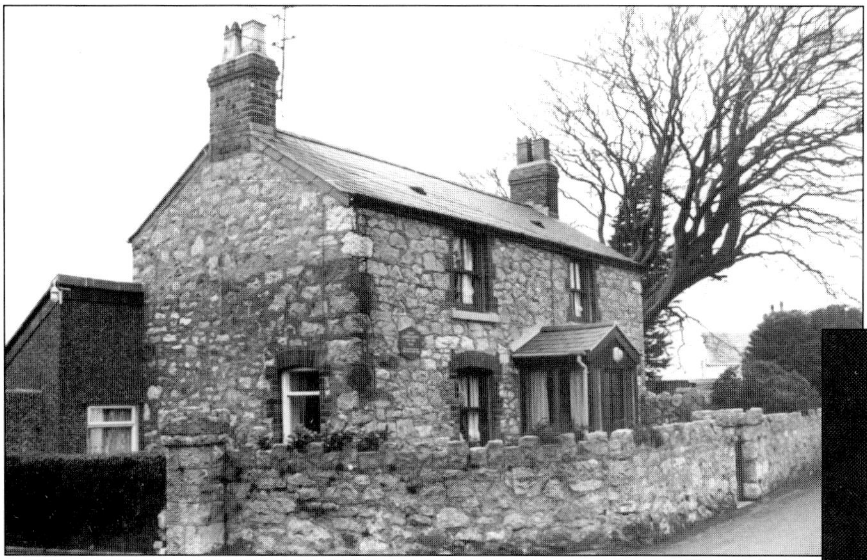

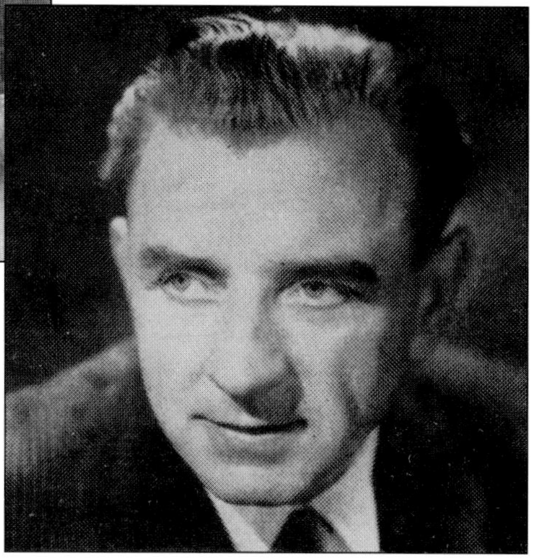

Welsh tenor David Lloyd stands legendary as one of the greatest singers to come out of Wales and probably the greatest to come out of North Wales. He was described in his day as the 'prince of tenors' and the 'Welsh ambassador of song'. Born the son of miner at Bryn Seiriol, Trelogan, in 1912 and brought up an orphan by a motherly sister, David showed extraordinary musical talent from the age of 12. His rendition of the song Bachgen Bach o Gymru (Little Boy from Wales) at his school concert in Trelogan became the talk of the neighbourhood for months.

After leaving school he became an apprentice joiner in Rhuddlan, devoting most of his spare time to singing at concerts and eisteddfodau. When early signs showed promise of a musical career, he entered the Guildhall School of Music in London in 1932, gaining the highest possible awards including a gold medal for best tenor.

Prize after prize fell into his lap and his reputation increased. He sang at the Royal Albert Hall promenade concerts and with the Sadler's Wells Opera, his foreign tours included America and Canada where packed houses would marvel at the quality and purity of tone in his voice. He once described how he would 'fix his gaze on one person in an audience and sing as if to that person alone'

During the 1950s and 60s he was kept busy with radio and television appearances and at the recording studios. David Lloyd gave pleasure to thousands of people during his career but remained devoted to his first love of singing in the village halls and churches of North Wales.

He died in 1969 after a fall at his home, he was 57. His records are as popular as ever today and he will always be remembered as one of the finest singers to emerge from what after all is the Land of Song. He is buried at Picton Cemetery and a plaque on his former home in Trelogan (pictured above) commemorates his memory.

Mostyn: A Hidden Heritage

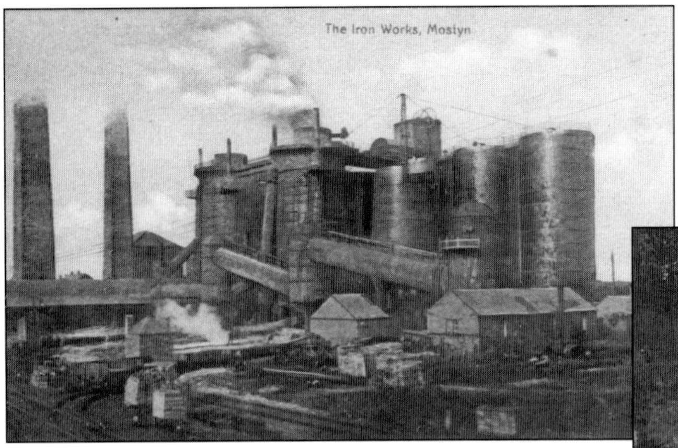

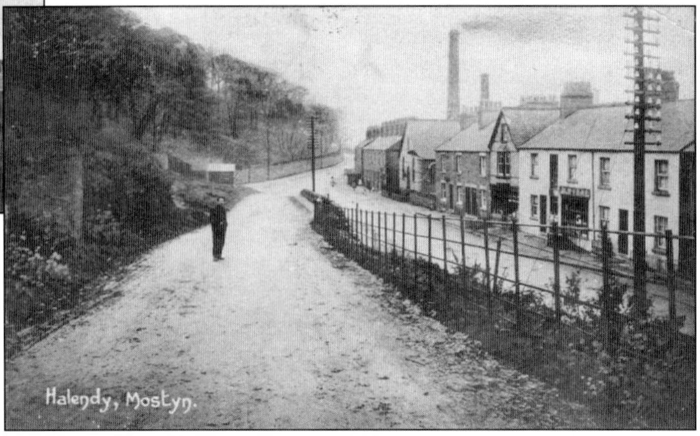

Mostyn is a village we all pass through on our journey to Holywell or Chester without taking a second glance and without really noticing it, believing it to be seemingly devoid of interest. But how wrong can you be about this closest-knit of communities?

This proud and ancient village is steeped in history - shipping has visited Mostyn Quay for centuries, the port was a highway for all goods in and out of Mostyn, as well as people, and up until the 1890s, the paddle steamer Swiftsure plied between Mostyn and Liverpool at a return fare of two shillings (10p).

Coal mining has also been a major industry at Mostyn, at one time employing 2,000 men. The largest mine was on the quayside at Mostyn Docks until flooding forced its closure in 1884, putting hundreds of men out of work at a stroke.

Another major industry was the Darwyn and Mostyn Ironworks, built around 1800 to satisfy the huge demand for iron created by the Napoleonic Wars. One of the primary reasons the ironworks site at Mostyn was chosen was the huge deposits of coal in the area which could easily be reduced to coke for the furnaces.

By virtue of stock market deceptions manipulated by people hoping to get rich quick, the ironworks was forced to close in 1964. Today, part of the site is occupied by Mostyn Docks and the Warwick International plant.

For such a small village, Mostyn once boasted an impressive array of shops. In Halendy at the bottom of Rhewl hill, pictured here in 1906, there existed a butchers, newsagents, general store and bicycle repair shop while Harry Parry's shop sold everything from meat to Zebo grate polish and paraffin.

Out of the 13 pubs once located at Mostyn, the most famous surviving pub must be the Lletty, a carved head over the doorway bears the inscription 'The Honest Man 1699'. It is reputed to have a tunnel connecting with the shore at the Dee which was once used by smugglers of a bygone age for their illicit trade in brandy, rum and tobacco.

Mostyn Ironworks pictured here in 1905 were built around 1800. So it can be seen that Mostyn has an historical pedigree to rival any village of its size in Wales.

Queen's Palace Reigns Supreme Over Rhyl...

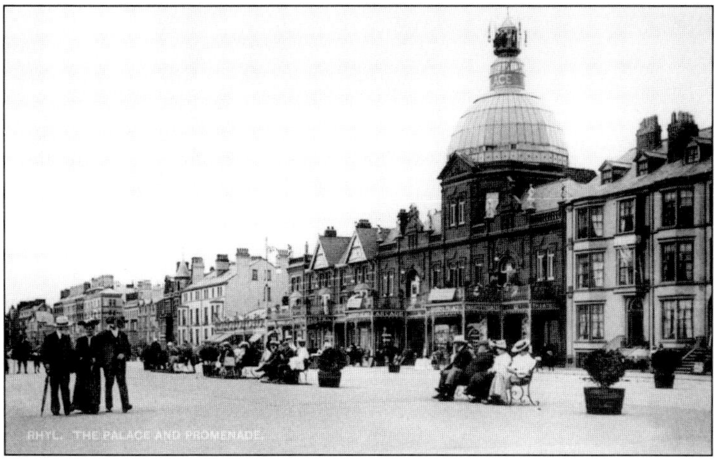

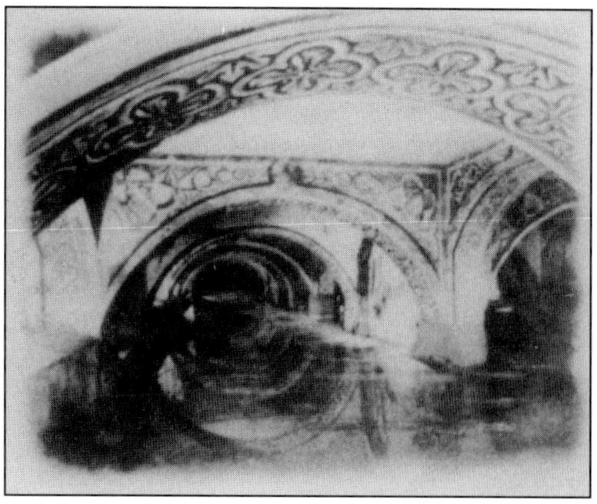

I am frequently asked about that glamorous era when Italian-attired gentlemen ferried visitors around on gondolas through the canals built under Rhyl's Queen Palace. So here is a potted history of Rhyl's once-greatest Victorian building that dominated the seafront skyline for a mere five years.

Built in 1892 and opened in 1902 by the Rhyl's Palace and Arcade Company , it was described as 'surpassing anything previously attempted in the history of Rhyl'. The Queens Palace was a luxurious four storey building accommodating a large theatre and ballroom which was reputedly the largest in Britain at that time. On the ground floor there was an amusement arcade and a spacious shopping complex containing an ornamental water fountain. Among the 35 shops therein you could purchase souvenirs, have your photo taken, your fortune told, you hair styled or watch hypnotically as cigarettes were rolled by hand.

For refreshments there were delicious Swiss cream cakes to buy or you could relax and reflect on the Queen's awesome structure at the coffee room or enjoy a meal at the airy restaurant. Open from 10.30am until 10.30pm, admission to the Queens was 1/6d (7½ p) and beneath the huge glass dome, visitors discovered a vast roof garden containing a variety of plants and a popular zoo house. Near to the entrance of the Venice attraction was a modern day lift that took you up to a small viewing platform above the dome at a height of 145 feet. When you reached the tower, a clear day provided the opportunity to enjoy views across to Snowdon, the Isle of Man, Liverpool and the hills of Ireland.

Beneath the Queens ground level was the Venice attraction which drew enormous crowds for an admission of 2d (1p) while a trip on the gondolas would set you back an extra penny. The Venice was essentially a representation of the famous Italian water city on a miniature scale. A poster at the time read: "Not only are the walls of the building adorned at great expense with faithful likeness of present-day Venetian scenes but even the eight double arches that span the walled-in waterways on which real gondolas are propelled by real Italians, are treated in a style that should satisfy most fastidious tastes." The fact is that these real Italians where just locally employed men dressed in appropriate clothing. The description continues, "Even the ceiling is star-spangled so that at night, while the hundred electric lamps are aglow, it is delightful to contemplate."

It must have been a rare privilege and an unforgettable sight for families on holiday to experience everything the Queen's Palace had to offer in what was an ageless and more glamourous period. Sadly the Queen's was destroyed by fire in 1907 but had it survived, it would possibly have developed into one of Britain's greatest attractions right here in Rhyl. The Queen's bowling alley, the Vanilla Lounge & Blush night clubs and the promenade entrance to the indoor market are today sited where the Queen's once stood.

A Bye-Di-Bye to the Old Days of Hi-Di-Hi

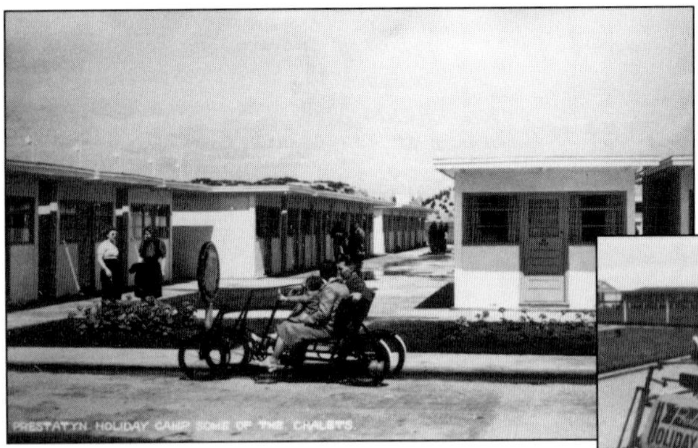

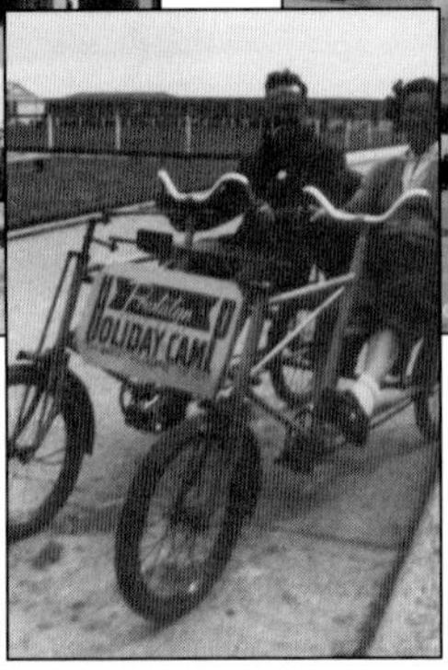

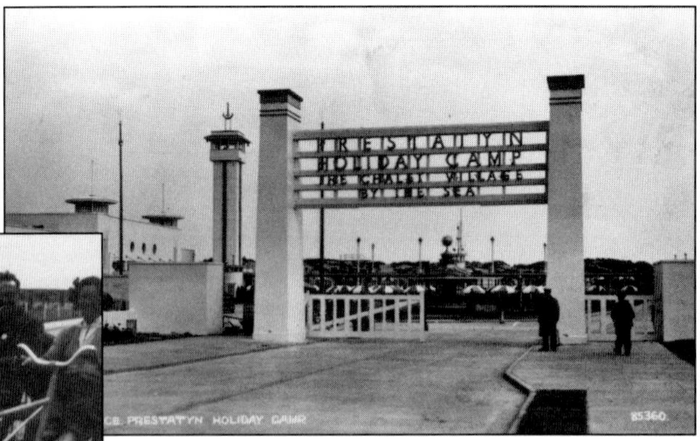

We all said a bye-di-bye to the very first holiday camp built in North Wales when it was sadly demolished in 2001 to make way for what is now Tower Gardens housing complex in Rhodfa Wyn. The camp's Hamlyn Tower, so evocative of the period became a Prestatyn landmark and an historic marker for the golden age of holiday camps, chalet maids, bluecoats, stage shows and dances.

Also known as the 'chalet village by the sea', Tower Beach was opened in 1939 by Lord Stamp, chairman of the LMS railway who jointly controlled the camp with Thomas Cook by way of a subsidiary company, British Holiday Estates.

The 58-acre camp was built to the design of architect W H Hamlyn of the LMS and a weeks stay in 1939 (including meals) was £3/3/6d (£3.18p). And for an extra charge, cheerful tea ladies with a trolley urn would greet campers with an early morning cuppa. The camp boasted 900 chalets holding a total of 2,000 guests. The colourful brochure verbosely declared 'Yes! it's almost like a holiday on the continent, clean, modern buildings surrounded by colourful chalets, a lavishly appointed swimming pool and Lido, tennis, bowls and a gymnasium, the finest ballroom in Wales and nurseries to take care of the toddlers.

"The free and easy, do-as-you-please atmosphere greets you as soon as you arrive...The first thing you notice is the number of flowers, they're literally everywhere in the camp, creating a wonderful South of France atmosphere and the fun doesn't stop when the sun goes down! Twice a week there's a first rate stage show, in addition you can dance every evening to the excellent orchestra in the ballroom and the Friday night fancy dress is one of the highlights of your stay."

On arrival, campers were greeted by 'Bluecoats' in reception with each child being given a camp badge. It was the Bluecoats job to arrange entertainment and competitions like donkey derby, knobbly knees, bathing beauty parades and 'Admiral of the Week' a Sunday event aimed at finding the best-looking man on the camp!

The 'lucky' winner would then be sat in a chair over the pool lathered in shaving cream, 'shaved' with a large wooden cutlass then a lever would be pulled, the chair would tilt and the "admiral" would be dunked in the swimming pool to roars of appreciation from the watching crowds.

A week 'all in' at the camp in 1965 was £9 and its camp slogan read: 'It's gay, it's great It's Prestatyn Holiday Camp in lovely North Wales.' It is my great belief that the camp's tower should have been left standing as a legacy and a fitting epitaph to Tower Beach's memory, success and popularity.

Telegraph Signalled the End of a Maritime Era

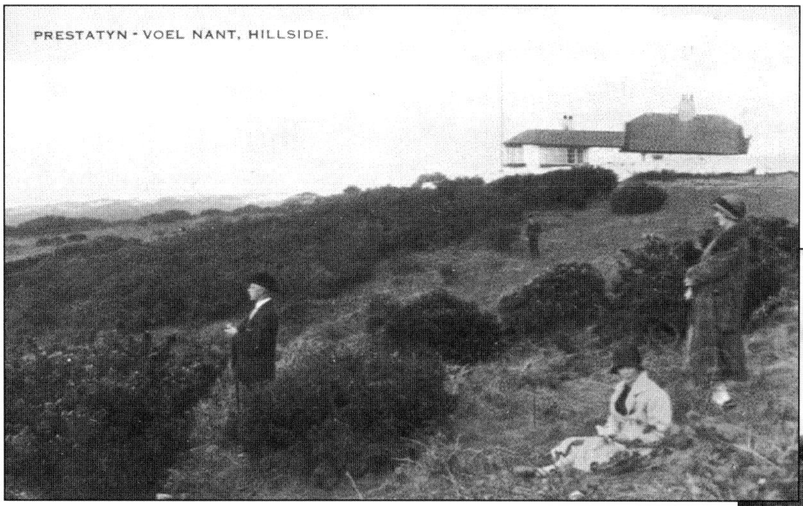

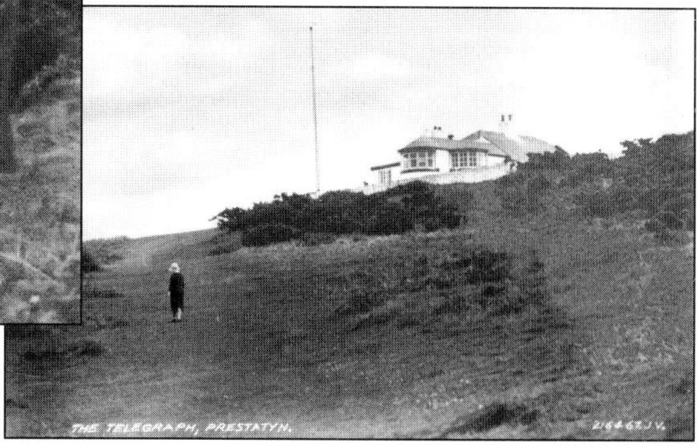

The picturesque old Voel Nant telegraph station, also known as the Coastguard and the Telegraph, stands on the hill above the road between Prestatyn and Gronant. The hillside was at one time a local beauty spot for sight-seeing, embracing the views of Gronant, Prestatyn, the Dee Estuary and beyond. At one time teas could be had here.

Voel Nant telegraph station building today is one of the more interesting historic buildings in the area. It was built in 1841 to establish a semaphore signalling service so advance warning could be given of merchant shipping sighted off Holyhead approaching Liverpool Bay, signalling stations at Holyhead mountain and Tower Buildings Liverpool would relay the messages. The windows of each station had small opening panes through which powerful telescopes could be driven to view the signals which where made by a chain and a lever mechanism. The signalling precision of the signalman was of a very high standard as a mistake had serious consequences and could prove fatal.

The last semaphore signal sent at Voel Nant was on November 24th 1869. Electric telegraph took over the following day. Outside Voel Nant boundary wall, on a stone slab to accommodate wheels, there was at one time a small warning cannon which fired rockets to notify the lifeboat at Gronant that a ship was in distress.

One of the worst disasters off the North Wales coast was that of the emigrant ship the Ocean Monarch which sank off Colwyn Bay through an accidental fire in 1848 with the loss of 178 lives. Fifty bodies were washed ashore near Prestatyn and were taken to Penisardre farmhouse stables, Prestatyn (where the shopping precinct is today) to await identification. Nine are buried in a churchyard in Abergele.

The scorched figurehead of the Ocean Monarch later drifted ashore at Rhos on Sea from where it was taken to Mochdre to be used as a wall decoration in the Mountain View Hotel. After Voel Nant ceased being a telegraph station it became a private house. An extension was built on to the building by the Pochin family who used it as a holiday home.

It was also lived in for 60 years by a Mrs Brewis who opened it up for teas during the summer months. She also made a variety of toffee and sweets, which she placed in glass dishes for visitors to savour and enjoy. Today the old Voel Nant telegraph station building is a private house, an ideal place to tell stories of sea life while enjoying the breath taking, embrace views and the unpolluted, salubrious air.

The telegraph station is pictured here on both postcards in the 1920s

When the Brass Bands Played, Tiddley-om-pom-pom...

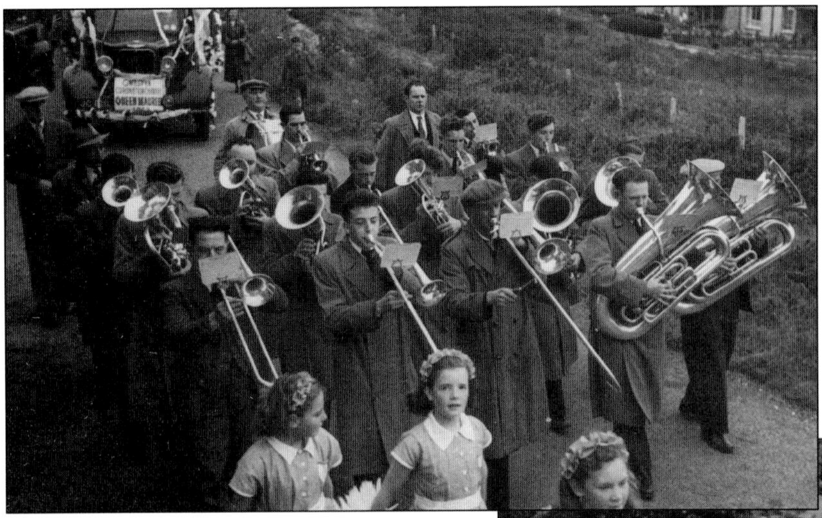

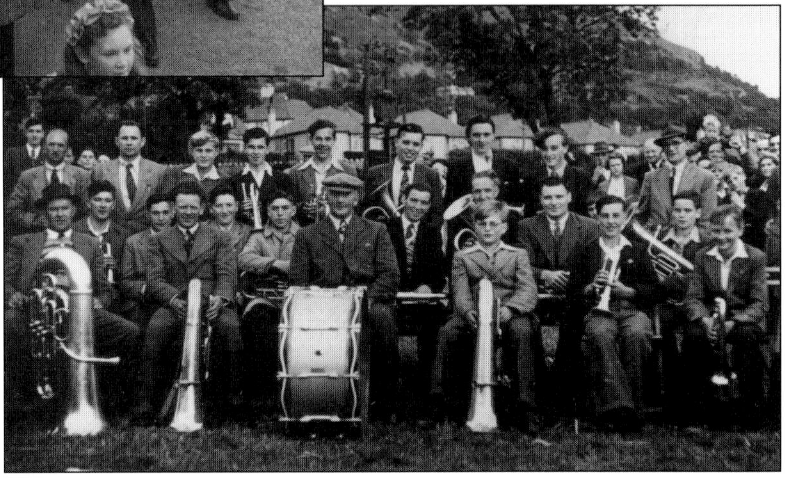

Our top photo shows Gwespyr Silver Band pictured in 1953 and you can almost hear them playing as they parade through the village in that year's carnival coronation for the Gwespyr Carnival Queen Maureen Thomas (no relation).

The carnival was an annual event the community of Gwespyr waited for with anticipation in the days when long hot summers were almost guaranteed for such events. Originally known as Gwespyr Brass Band when they were formed in the 1920s, they soon gained popularity for their concerts and charity work.

At that time they practiced in a room above the Mason's Arms pub in the village under their bandleader Edward Ellis. They changed their name to Gwespyr Silver Band when Eric Hopkins from Bagillt took over as their new bandleader in the 1950s. At this time they were then practising in a garage alongside the Talacre Arms pub.

On warm sunny days they played outside the Inn to customers and passing visitors. The proudest day in the band's history came when they won the North Wales Brass Band competition at the Arcadia Theatre, Llandudno, in the 1950s - a treasured memory the surviving members of the band fondly remember.

Gwespyr Silver Band - like all things that are good - came to an end in the early 1960s but the Band's instruments were not lost, they were eventually transferred to the town band at nearby Holywell.

Bottom Picture: Gwespyr Silver Band 1951
Top Row L - R: Dave Holland, Will Lloyd, Neville Lloyd, Dave Kenny, Keith Parry, Unknown, Barry Evans, Vic Bagshaw, Unknown; Middle Row L - R: Unknown, Freddie Mills, Les Mullock, Albert Hughes, Jock Morgan, Sam Hurst, Unknown, Terry Malloney; Front Row L - R: Eric Davies, Tommy Davies, Bob 'The Drummer' Roberts, Derek Lloyd, Gordon Wheeler, Terence Jones.

Kings of the High Street

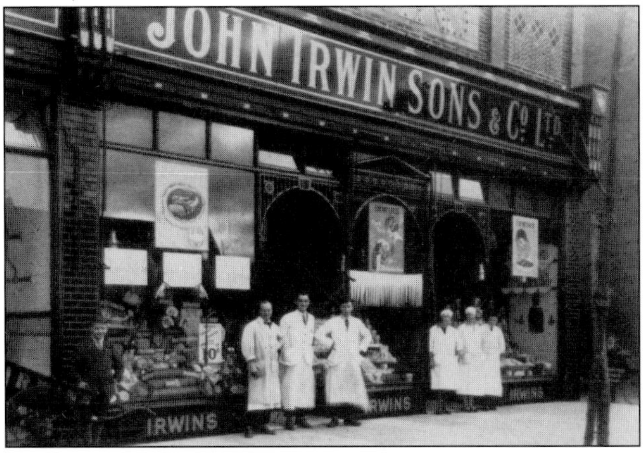

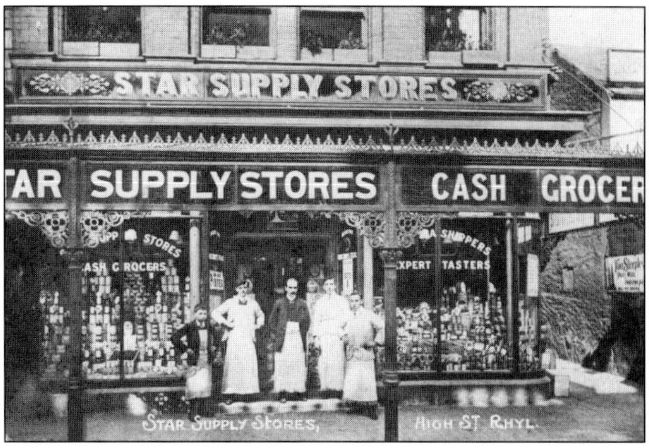

With the demise of the larger and better-known grocers shops in our High Streets, these forerunners of today's supermarkets became legends for their service and customers were deemed of paramount importance. They were respected, shown unrivalled courtesy, and treated as individuals in an unhurried, friendly shopping environment - qualities sadly missing from the supermarkets of today.

Many of you will still remember those well established High Street grocers such as Irwins, the Star Supply Stores, E B Jones, the Co-op, Coopers and the Maypole. Names that supplied and served the everyday needs of every family.

Halcyon days so very different from today. Fridges were unknown, the cold marble slab in the pantry had to suffice. Pre-packed food and self-service were also unknown, everything was either sold from sacks, barrels or tins. Butter and margarine that came in barrels had to be patted into shape with wooden paddles on a marble slab on the counter before being wrapped and bacon was sliced by hand on a large slicing machine.

Tea, coffee, sugar, flour, salt, cheese, spices, biscuits and the rest of the daily needs were weighed then wrapped when bought, and liquids such as vinegar were poured into jugs you took along to the shop. For the convenience of the customers, stores would often provide chairs to sit on while their orders were being made up.

The aromas as you entered the grocers from the freshly baked bread, ground coffee and spices were something to behold and a lasting memory of your visit. One assistant who worked for EB Jones, Rhyl, many years ago told me the aroma that filtered through the shop was sometimes enhanced by placing a metal lid covered with coffee beans on a paraffin heater in the back room.

Another distinctive feature from those evocative days was the delivery service to your doorstep by young boys on bikes, some baskets on the front were so laden with groceries that a second boy with a rope helped pull the bike. These youngsters - out in all weathers - were a lifeline to the elderly and infirm.

In the early 1900s these delivery boys earned the princely sum of five shillings (25p) for a 12 hour, six day week. The Shops Act of 1911 eventually introduced holidays and early closing days. The disappearance of these pre-supermarket grocers came with the advent of convenience shopping and pre-packed food in the 1960s. Perhaps some modern day supermarkets could learn from their forerunners regarding customer care!

Left Picture: 1921: Irwins at the bottom of High Street Prestatyn, today the site of Ethel Austin.

Right Picture: 1910: Star Supply Stores in High Street Rhyl. Boots the Chemist is located here today.

Frozen Fragments of Time

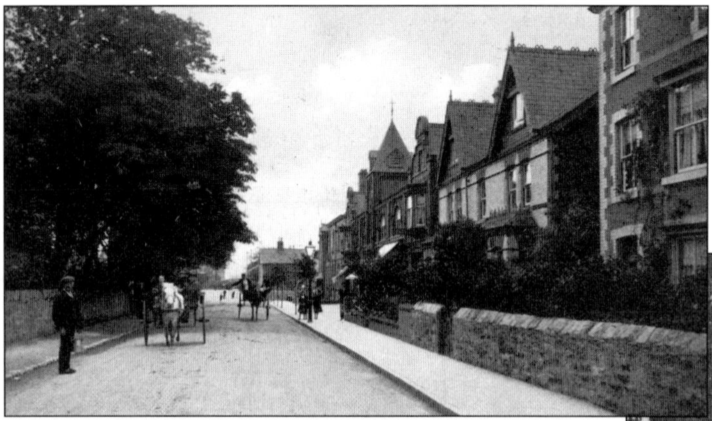

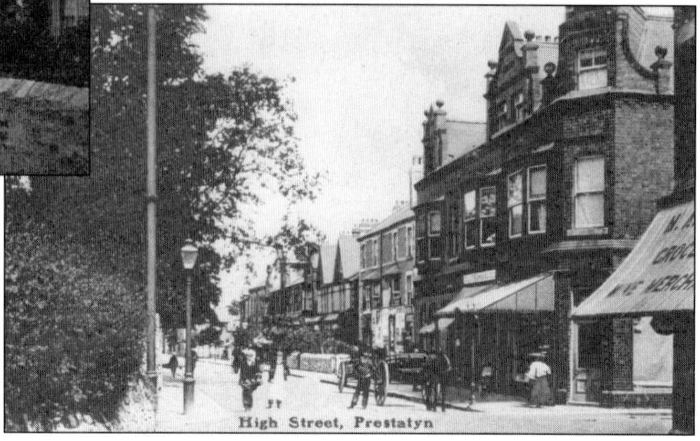

The owner with his horse and cart on the right are a an idyllic study in social history as they stand in eternal wait posing for the camera on the corner of High Street and Nant Hall Road in the summer of 1915. Prestatyn's post office and general store was at the time located here until they were burnt to the ground in a huge fire in 1899. A new larger and more modern post office was built in 1915 (where it still is today in Kings Avenue).

The Card Warehouse is on this corner today. The trees, bushes and the stone wall on the left are where Woolworths was to be built in 1934, note the gas lamp on the left. The Town Council employed lamp lighters who travelled around the town with a taper on the end of a pole to light the mantles of the gas lamps every night, and again in the early morning to put them out. They were paid ten shillings (£4.50) a year.

On one night in 1916 during the first World War, Prestatyn's gas supply was disconnected putting the whole town in darkness as the police had been informed that Zeppelins were patrolling the skies, fortunately no Zeppelins appeared that night.

Electricity came to Prestatyn when the formal inauguration of electric power took place in 1927 when it was switched on by Councillor Clement Hughes, chairman of the electric committee. A tranquil residential scene when the only traffic in the High Street was horsedrawn is faithfully captured of the middle of High Street, Prestatyn, in 1907 (left).

The building on the right with the spire was Prestatyn Town Hall opened in 1900. As early as 1910 films were being shown here by pioneer cinematographer Saronie, who later converted it to the Scala Cinema.

The neatly built wall on the right is where Jeff's Fruit Market is today, the houses standing further along are today the premises of the National Westminster Bank and Numark Pharmacy.

The Oak trees on the left stood on land where 16th century Penisardre farmhouse once stood. Up until the late 1930s cattle were still being herded over the railway bridge and through the busiest part of town into Penisardre much to the annoyance of the horse-drawn vehicles.

Premises along here today include: the Abbey National, Rumours Cafe and Cumberlidges the Jewellers. Penisardre was demolished in 1964.

A Village that had the Abbey Habit...

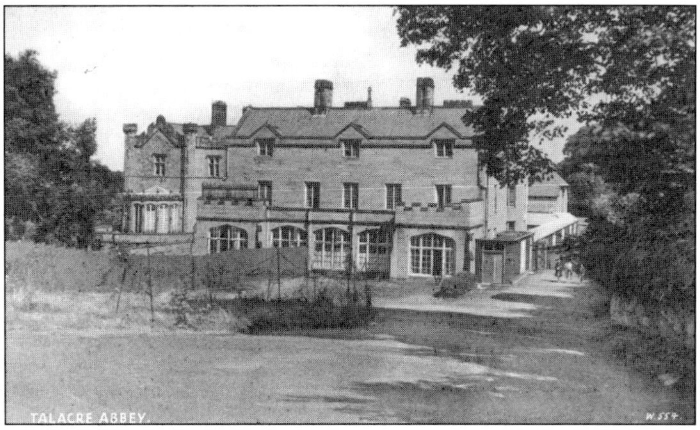

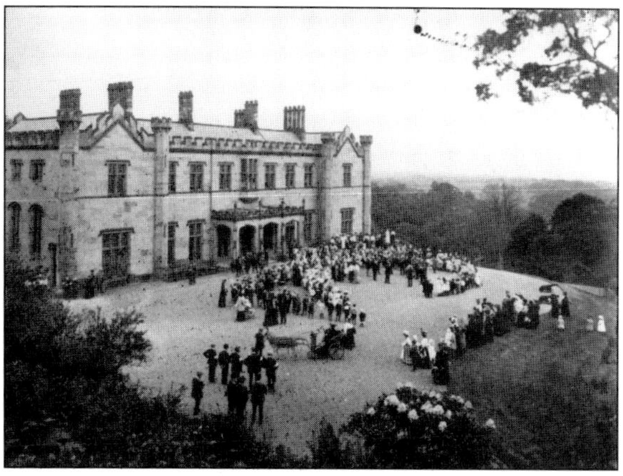

Steeped in history, Talacre Hall in the confines of Gronant is now a shadow of its former glory. It had been occupied by the Mostyn family since the late 15th century and is reputed to stand on the site of a fortified minor castle. The early Mostyns improved their status and increased their wealth and land holdings through marrying heiresses from Oxford, Essex, Norfolk and Scotland, without love or romance ever entering their relationships.

Talacre Hall had an indoor staff of 50 including maids, butlers and footmen. Due to the age and unfit state of the old Hall in which to raise a family, Sir Edward Mostyn had it taken down in 1825 and architect Thomas Jones of Chester was commissioned to plan a new building.

But when the mansion was partly built in 1827 it was destroyed by fire, and at a cost of £70,000 it was rebuilt in 1829 and became a home to be envied. The new Hall had over 40 rooms with its own private family chapel and was idyllically situated, surrounded by lawns and woodlands, courtyards and riding stables. Water-lillied lakes for boating and fishing were also on the land as were spacious gardens with huge heated glasshouses producing grapes, peaches and orchids, along with vegetable gardens and orchards.

Along the drive to Gronant were coach houses, dovecotes, kennels and smithies. On high ground, a stone summerhouse was built with excellent views of the Dee Estuary to Anglesey.

Talacre Hall remained in the Mostyn family until they were crippled by death duties in 1920 when two bereavements in quick succession forced them to sell the 3,600 acre estate triggering a succession of unfortunate circumstances. In a letter to the Independent in 1933, a member of the Mostyn family described how he felt a curse had been placed on his family because they had sold the estate. He told how his uncle, on leaving the estate, went big game hunting in Africa and died in an aircraft accident whilst his heir was trampled to death by a mad horse in Kenya and both successors had died young.

The building officially became an Abbey when it was taken over by an enclosed community of Benedictine nuns in 1920 who added a churchyard and a bell tower to the building. In 1988 the nuns left for more manageable accommodation in Chester.

Today the owner of Talacre Hall, Graham Jones is sympathetically restoring it to its former glory, while the surrounding land is owned by Jeff Mound of Gwespyr.

Right: This picture shows celebrations of the relief of Ladysmith at Talacre Hall in 1900

Left: The entrance to Talacre Abbey in the 1930s

Rhyl's Fraudulent Heiress Violet Charlesworth

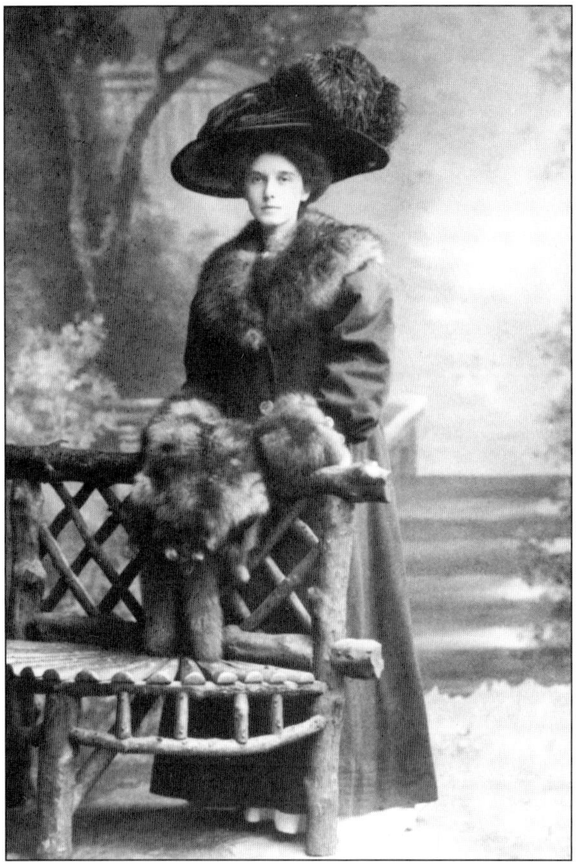

The captivating story of 24 year old fraudulent heiress Violet Charlesworth is one of the most fascinating and colourful stories from Rhyl's rich historic and turbulent past.

In 1907 Violet Charlesworth came from the Midlands with her mother, father, eighteen year old sister Eileen and chauffeur (believed to be her husband) to live near the Foryd in Rhyl. Temptress and hoaxer Violet Charlesworth, who captured newspaper headlines throughout Britain with her seductive alluring lifestyle was said to be a woman who knew what she wanted, and always achieved in obtaining what she wanted by using her seductive charm, beauty and elegance, a rarity in a woman in those intensely class-conscious Edwardian days that she was living in, when women were not yet emancipated. Violet was often seen around Rhyl in the most luxurious and expensive cars of the day, constantly seen wearing her striking red motor-cloak, with her beloved pet dogs by her side.

Violets mother led people to believe that Violet was the god-daughter of General Gordon of Khartoum and that she was to inherit £100,000 from his estate on her 25th birthday. Violet soon became something of an admiration in Rhyl, having local businessmen falling over each other to befriend this beautiful young "heiress." A Rhyl doctor who she befriended fell for her charms and lent her £5,000 promising to pay him back after her "inheritance". She also extorted £10,000 from a London stockbroker promising him also to be paid on her "inheritance".

The Charlesworths found that living near the Foryd had become too noisy for them due to the passing of heavy shipping traffic and moved to "Boderw" an impressive small mansion near St Asaph where they lived from 1907 to 1909. However on January 2nd 1909 a week before Violets so called "inheritance" Miss Charlesworth had supposedly lost control of her car at Penmaenbach, Penmaenmawr and gone over the cliffs into the sea below.

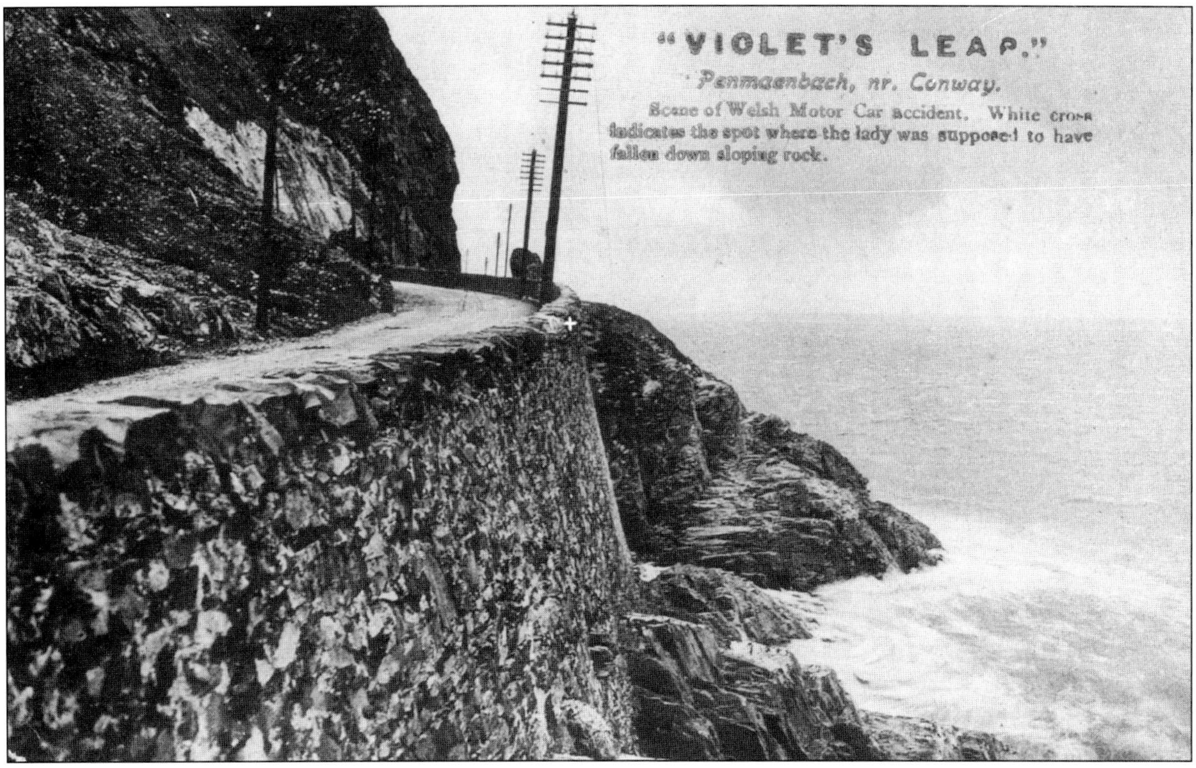

Disbelieving police were later to search the length of Britain for her after enquiries discovered she had debts of £27,000. Her story made newspaper headlines and her name became infamous throughout the country, the whole of Britain was alerted to the red cloak she always used to wear and soon there were "red-cloak" sightings. It was said that ladies with red coats gave up wearing them to avoid embarrassment.

Eventually Violet Charlesworth was found very much alive and well living under a false name in Oban, West of Scotland, when she was on bail awaiting charges to be made against her she earned a living at the "top of the bill" in many London theatres by simply appearing as herself in her red cloak while a speaker narrated her adventurous life. Violet Charlesworth and her mother were later arrested, charged and in court both were sentenced to five years hard labour, later reduced on appeal to three years.

The location at Penmaenbach where Violet Charlesworth faked her accident is now known as "Violets Leap" and a postcard was produced at the time of Penmaenbach printed with a small white cross indicating the scene of Violets faked car crash and disappearance.

Death and Mayhem at Wales' Biggest Army Base

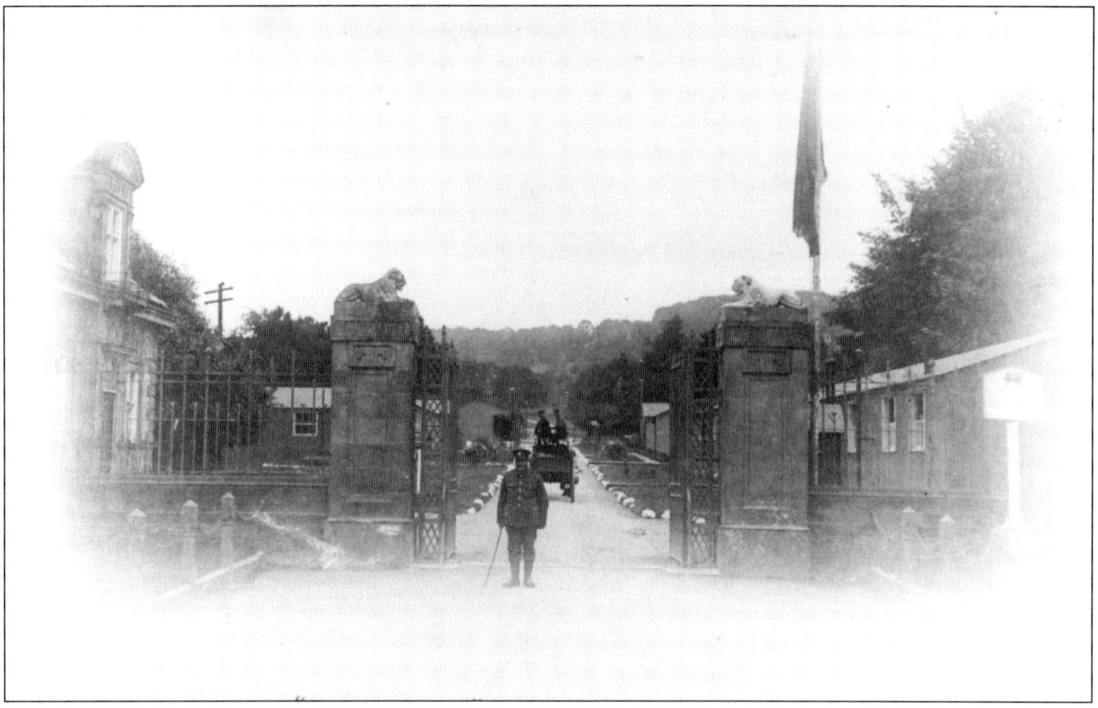

The greatest ill fated local tragedy to occur during the final years of the First World War and today firmly established in the history books was the Kinmel Park Camp Riots of 1919.

Built in 1915 without barriers separating the camp from the countryside, Kinmel Camp was the largest of its kind in Wales accommodating its own post office, theatre, cinema, church, bakery, YMCA building, civilian owned shops and specially-constructed standard gauge railway passenger and goods service to carry heavy items of equipment, coal, supplies and catering.

The camp's main objective was to train soldiers for active service towards the end of the First World War. However, 20,000 Canadian soldiers crammed into the camp became increasingly frustrated by the overcrowded conditions and delay in their demobilisation.

On top of this there was a shortage of fuel with many of the men having to sleep on the wooden floors of their huts without blankets or heating. There was also a lack of food and reduction in pay preventing the men from obtaining entertainment, tobacco, toiletries and alcohol.

The policy of shipping home conscripts and married men first added to the men's discomfort and had already caused minor disturbances which sparked rioting and looting of the stores with furniture and windows being smashed.

Rhyl shopkeepers, on hearing what was happening worked frantically to board up their shops, fearing the rioting soldiers would head for the town. A small minority did journey to Rhyl for a night's drinking and when they returned to the camp drunk, a serious confrontation started and hand-to-hand fighting took place with bayonets being used by soldiers defending the camp.

A corporal was hacked in the face and then later died in hospital. By this time 1,000 men, many with rifles, were on the rampage with one defender being shot attempting to make an arrest. This soon led to a shoot-out resulting in the rioting soldiers being subdued and pushed back hoisting a white flag.

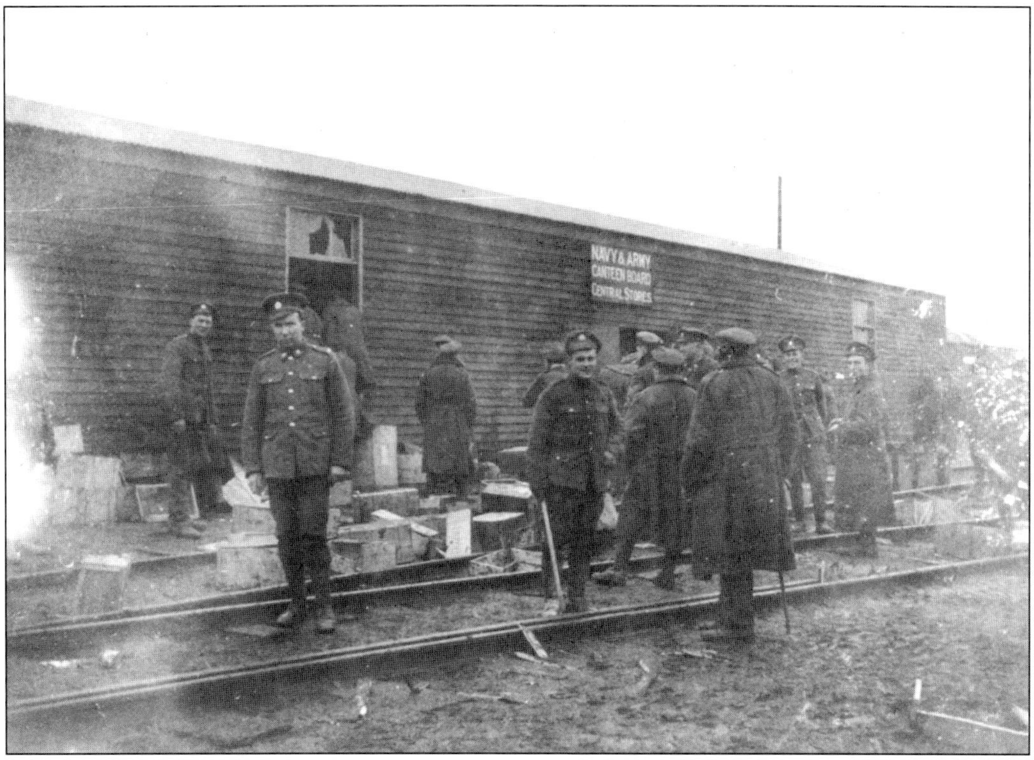

Following the riots five men had been killed, two by bayonet and three by bullets. Seventy men were arrested and charged with mutiny. At a court martial most of them served terms of hard labour and imprisonment. An open verdict was returned on the men who died, no death sentences were carried out.

The Canadian men who died at Kinmel Camp along with another 80 men who died in a flu epidemic that broke out that time are buried at Bodelwyddan's Marble Church cemetery. Each gravestone is carved with a maple leaf and the soldier's name, regiment and number. A memorial stone is inscribed with the words 'To the memory of the Canadian soldiers who died at Kinmel Camp during the Great War'

It is said that there was a great 'cover-up' regarding the men who died of influenza, many believing that the doctor who treated the men was a German sympathiser and that it was the medicine that caused their deaths. The doctor's German background was eventually revealed and he was later shot.

Kinmel Park Camp was rebuilt in 1939 to accommodate conscripts and it became an Artillery Camp when the Second World War started. It is now used as a training camp mainly by Army Cadets.

Previous Page: Entrance to Kinmel Camp 1918

Above: Army and Navy Stores, canteen and central stores were looted with furniture and windows being smashed seen here after the riots in 1919.

A Unique Glimpse into Prestatyn's Past Life...

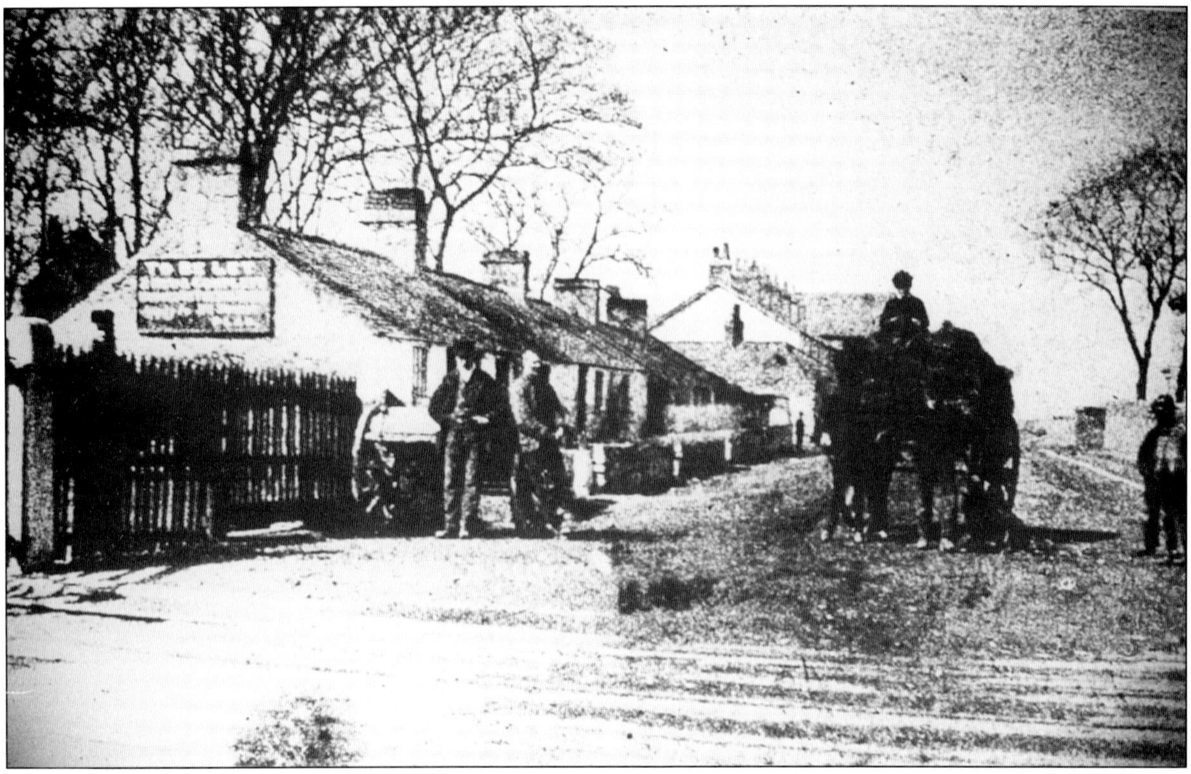

These rare and historic photographs of Prestatyn have never before been published and are seen here for the first time. The top photograph is dated 1878 and is the earliest-known view of Prestatyn as a village looking down Bastion Road from where Offa's Tavern is today.

The horse and cart cautiously approaches to cross the railway's level crossing which was abolished in 1897. The railway cottages on the left were demolished in 1897 to make way for the approach to the new road bridge and alterations to the railway station.

It is interesting to note that the road bridge over the railway was once known as the Cart Bridge, due to the number of horses and carts crossing over it. Prior to the cottages being built the land here was known as "Prestatyn Common". During the middle of the 1800s simple village sports were held here when crowds gathered to watch the men of Prestatyn and surrounding districts participate in the sports which consisted of trials of strength, jumping competitions and 'pitch and toss'. (Tossing a coin in the air and betting on which side it would land). Bare knuckle fighting also sometimes took place, that is if the police didn't arrive first! Today the splendidly built Victoria Hotel is located where the cottages once stood.

Evocative of the period, the photograph on the opposite page is of the top of Prestatyn High Street in 1908 when the population of Prestatyn was only 1,700 (Today's estimated population is 17,000). The romantically built cottages seen here were very characteristic of old Prestatyn, running the length of both sides of High Street. The white washed cottages were known as Pendre Cottages.

Grenville Williams came into possession of Pendre cottages in 1880, his great-uncle Edward Jones purchased these cottages when he was a policeman in Prestatyn. ET Williams, the councillor and popular headmaster at the old VP school in Bastion Road

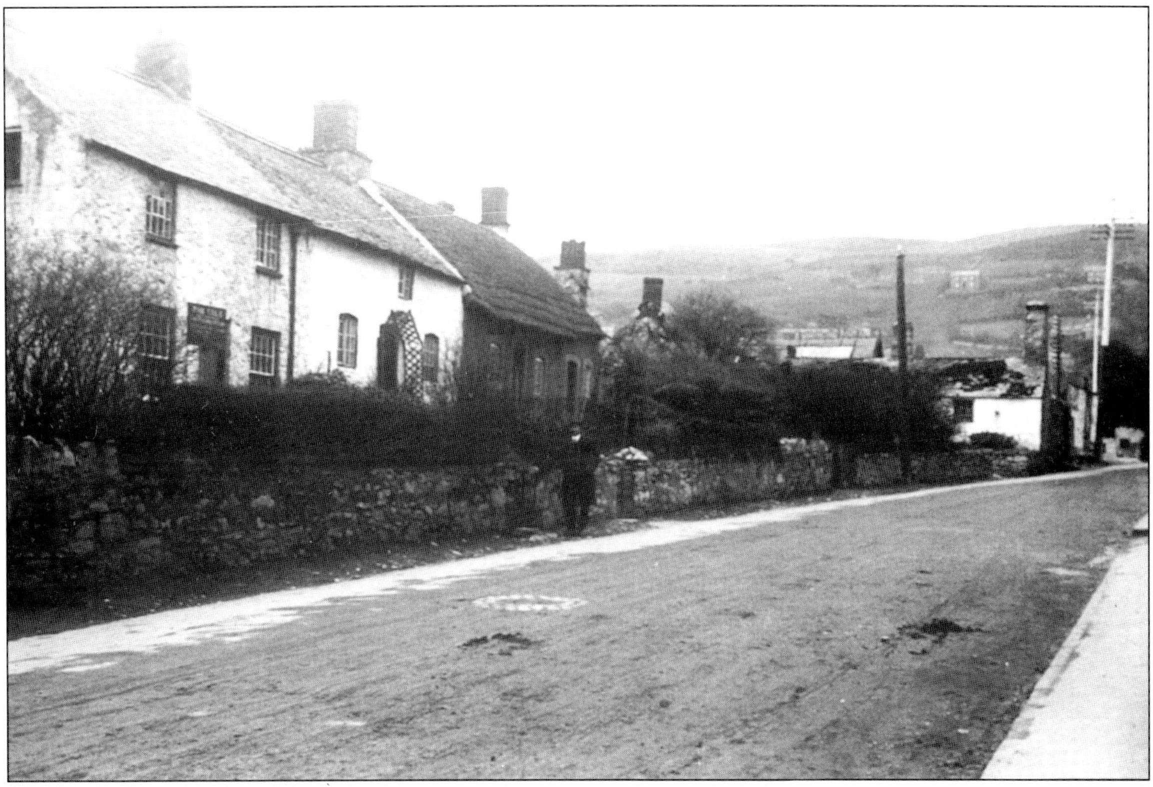

(where the Suhail Indian restaurant is today) spent his childhood days at these cottages, he later built Priory house building (where Bargain Booze is today).

Ann Ellis, who occupied Pendre Cottages, had the most magnificent singing voice in Prestatyn and she always called in her son Pugh by singing his name, her dulcet tones were heard all through the High Street. Sadly Pugh was killed as a Soldier during the First World War. Pendre Cottages, the last vestiges of old Prestatyn, were demolished in 1958.

When the thatched roofed cottages were demolished in 1934 a hoard of 519 silver coins were discovered in the chimney dating back to the reign of Elizabeth I (1558-1603) James I (1603-1625) and Charles I (1625-1649). An inquest on the hoard was held and the coroner's verdict was that the former resident of the cottage hid them around 1643 for safekeeping and therefore declared them as treasure trove. The coins today are kept at the National and British Museums. Complaints were made about residents from these cottages throwing waste water into the street and the coal burning house fires filling the street with smoke and soot. Today Powells the jewellers and Morrice-Evans opticians are located where these cottages once stood.

Tom Brooks is the man seen standing by the gates of the cottages, in 1912 he built a garage where Tegid Jones the undertakers is today. It was known as Prestatyn Motors, this photograph was taken by Saronie, manager of the Scala Cinema.

Our Links With a Famous Crime of Passion

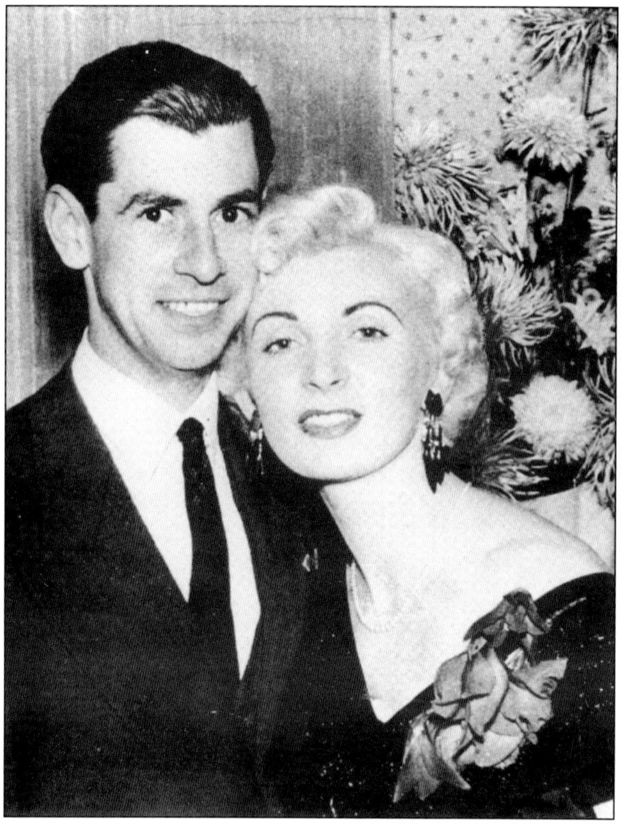

One of the most infamous crimes of passion during the post-war years was the Ruth Ellis murder case Ruth Ellis became the last woman to be hanged in this country after she shot to death her wealthy racing car driver playboy lover David Blakeley.

Ruth, an attractive 28-year-old platinum blonde night club hostess with a bubbly character, was born in 1926 at 74 West Parade, Rhyl as Ruth Neilson, the fourth child of musician Arthur and his Jewish wife Bertha. At the age of 13, Ruth was unlike the attractive woman she grew up to be, she was skinny, short sighted with lank hair.

Ruth's father earned his living on the transatlantic liners, moving to Rhyl because it was convenient to board the liners at nearby Liverpool. When Ruth's father lost his job due to the decline of the Liverpool shipping trade the family moved to London in 1941. Ruth's father found work as a chauffeur with a flat that went with the job, and 15-year-old Ruth found work at the Oxo factory.

When Ruth was in her twenties, she began working as a nightclub hostess at London's Court Club, it was here that she met 41-year-old dental surgeon George Ellis, a regular at the club and a dedicated alcoholic. Ruth's description of him was as a "mad dentist who told so many tales he came to believe in them. He used to buy me Champagne and spend a lot of money on me, hiring cars to frequently take me out for drives."

Ruth realised that George Ellis could provide her with money and the social status for which she yearned, their relationship grew and they were married in 1950, he was later fired from his work as a dental surgeon due to his drinking bouts.

In 1951 Ruth gave birth to a baby girl naming her Georgina. After the baby was born Ruth and George split up. Ruth returned to the world she knew and in 1953 she was made manageress of the Little Club, Brompton, with a rent-free flat above the premises.

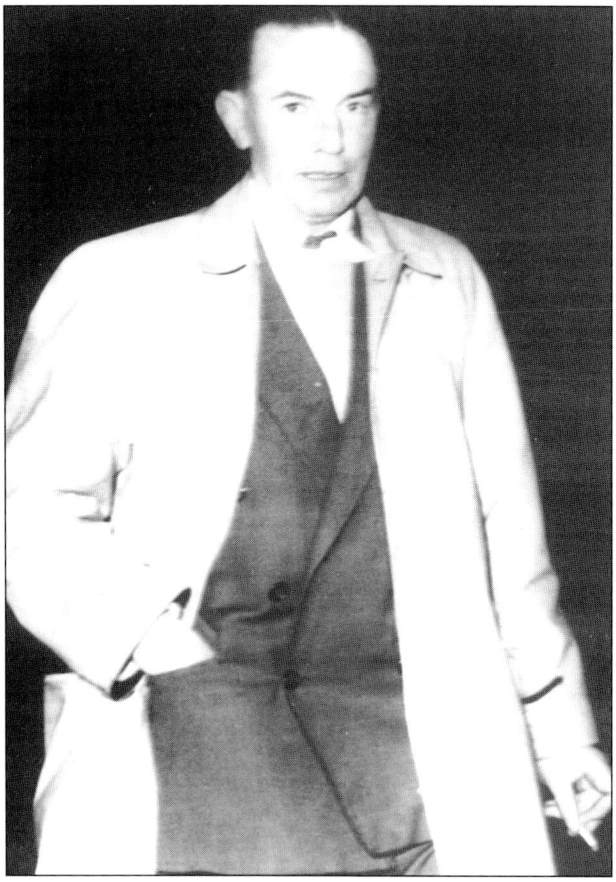

One night in 1954 while she was a guest at the Court Club she met David Blakeley, she recalls it was flattering to have a professional and educated man lusting after her, and just one month later he moved into Ruth's flat with her. After their divorce in 1955, George Ellis sank deeper in alcoholism and ended up killing himself in a hotel room.

Ruth and Blakeley's affair was stormy as he was an unfaithful lover, in the end the womanising Blakeley walked out on Ruth after forcing her to have an abortion. David Blakeley, a pampered, spoilt layabout from a wealthy family often beat Ruth when he was drunk, but she clung to the obsession that he really loved her.

Consumed with anger and blind fury because David Blakeley had failed to keep a date and had been avoiding her calls, Ruth Ellis took a Smith and Wesson revolver out of her bag and emptied the six-chambered gun into the love-rat as he was leaving the Magdalane pub, in north London.

At the Old Bailey it took the jury just 14 minutes to convict Ruth of murder. Ruth did not appeal against the sentence as she believed along with her legal team she would be reprieved. Her sentence sparked outrage and in 1957 the law was changed to allow a defence of diminished responsibility in a crime of passion. In a letter to Blakeley's mother from her cell in Holloway Prison, Ruth wrote 'I shall die loving your son and you should feel content that his death has been repaid, goodbye'.

Ruth Ellis was given the tot of brandy she was promised and walked the short steps from her cell to the room next door where she was hanged by Albert Pierrepoint, who described Ruth Ellis as 'The bravest of women, she went to the scaffold with calm dignity'.

The Ruth Ellis story was made into the 1985 film "Dance With a Stranger"

Previous Page: Ruth Ellis and her lover David Blakeley.

Above: Ruth's husband George.

Prestatyn Carnival is Always a Magical Event

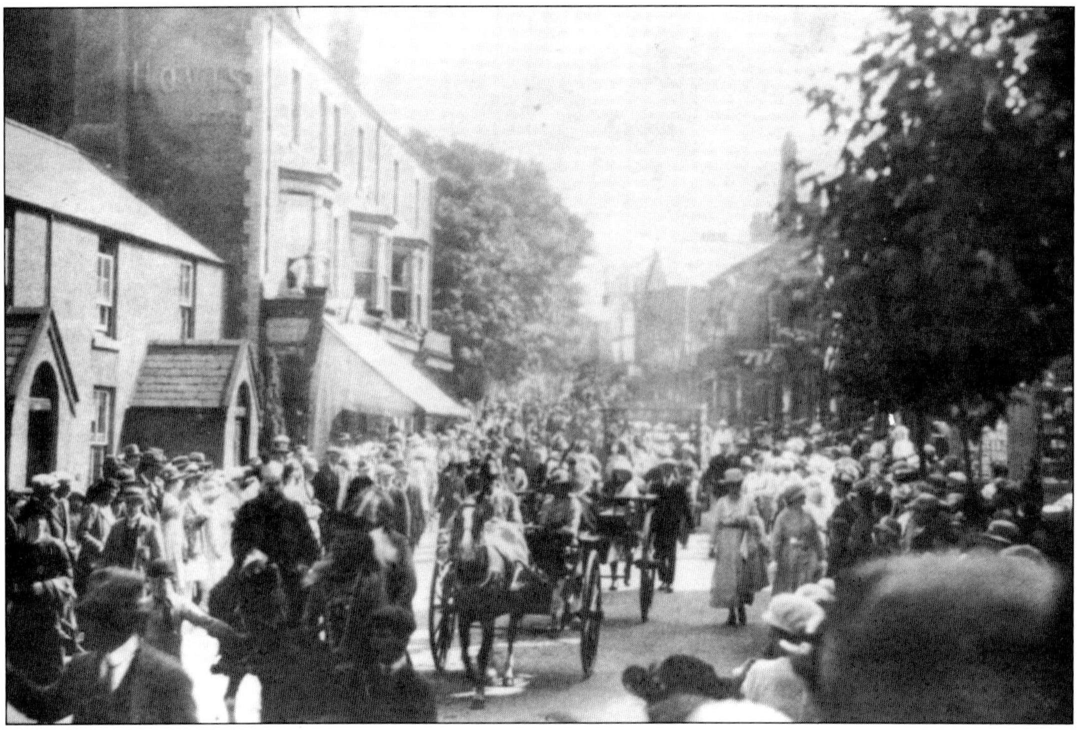

One of the largest and most popular events in North Wales continues to delight with its usual yearly pomp, ceremony and colour. It was back in 1921 when the carnival began its history as a celebration of the peace that followed the First World War.

The very first Carnival Queen was Gwyneth Dowell in 1922, with Margaret Williams being the first Miss Prestatyn in 1935. The carnival activities ceased during the second war, but were resumed again in 1950 when the festivities committee was founded by Lavinia Davies with her husband Ivor as secretary.

The committee organised a May Day and a Rose Day the following August. The post-war Carnival Queen was Hilary Kay, with two sisters Rita and Ursula Furber the first Prestatyn May Queen and Rose Queen respectively.

In 1951 May Day was held as usual but the Rose Day was incorporated in the town council's Festival Fortnight. The success of the Festival Fortnight inspired the festivities committee not only to organise the usual May Day but also Prestatyn's first carnival week since the war. In 1952 the name of the Festivities Committee was changed to that of the Prestatyn Carnival Association.

To concentrate all efforts on Carnival Week it was decided to hold no May Day in 1956 and none have been held since, the last May Queen being Sylvia Jones in 1955. Rose Day became Carnival Day and no Rose Queens have been elected since, Sandra Smith was crowned the last Rose Queen in 1958.

In 1956, for the first jazz time bands, morris dancers and entertaining troupes were introduced in the carnival week parade. Valerie Kay was elected the first post-war Miss Prestatyn, a title which was to only last a further year. The last-ever Miss Prestatyn title was held by Yvonne Lumsden in 1957.

Up until 1952 10-foot-tall stilt walker and local personality - Jimmy Oliver was to be seen in every carnival parade as was J.W. Playle who will be long remembered as a mounted marshal, resplendent in shining brass helmet and uniform on his horse at the head of the carnival procession also up until 1952.

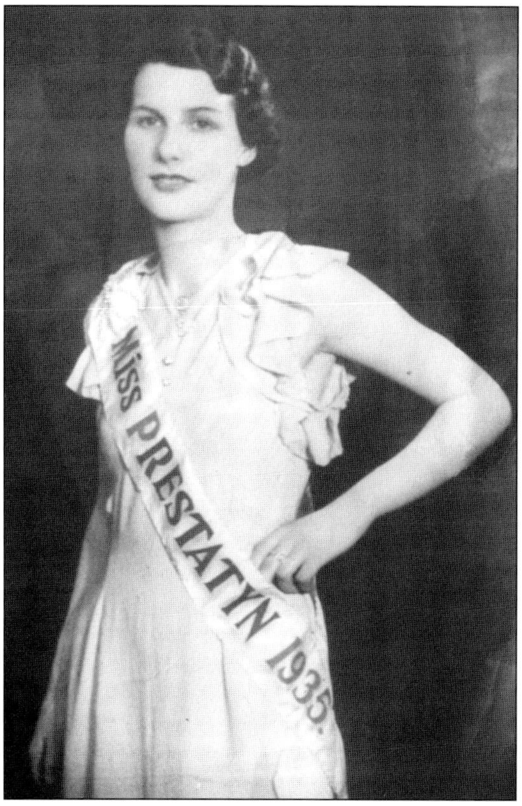

There was to be no carnival street procession in 1966 due to lack of money. This made people realise what they were missing and in 1967 the carnival was revived, with interest being shown by local organisations and shopkeepers. It was also in 1967 that the then Welsh heavyweight champion Carl Gizzi of Rhyl, crowned the two Empresses of Carnival.

Let us hope that Prestatyn Carnival continues to grow and that the sun always shines on what is a very popular and memorable event.

Previous Page: The first Prestatyn Carnival procession, looking up High Street from where Woolworths is today, in 1922. The building on the left with the two porches is where The Pantry Café is today.

Above: The very first "Miss Prestatyn" in 1935, Margaret Williams, who worked at the Chocolate Box in Prestatyn High Street (located where the Jewellery Box is today).

Remembering the Fun, But Bumpy, Tally Ho

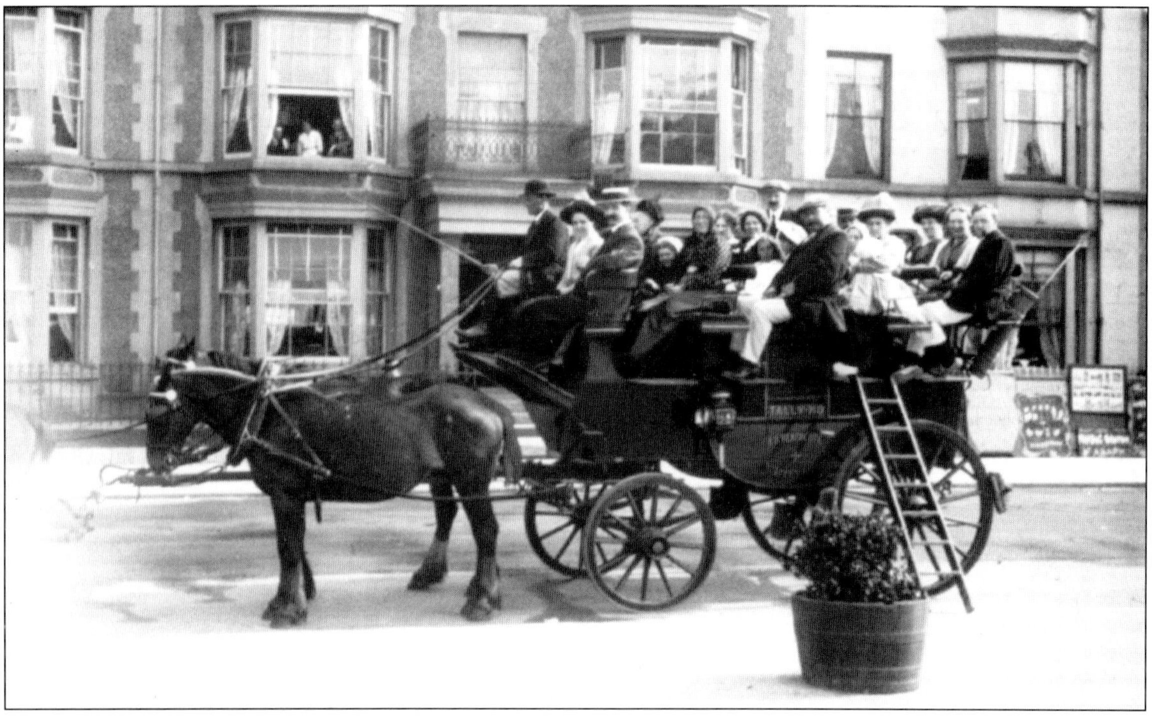

Thundering along the roads in and around Rhyl during the early 1900s and today resembling a relic from an old western film was this four horse-driven coach known as the "Tally Ho". Evoking a time when scenic country trips were part of the seaside holiday in Rhyl - along with long hot summers, picnics in meadows, food wasn't fast and clothes were quite sombre. This popular and exciting form of modern day transport for visitors and day trippers to Rhyl during the summer months stood on Rhyl promenade preparing to ferry passengers for an exhilarating journey to the local attractions for a return fare of three shillings (15p.)

Bookings for the scenic country trips with F and J Heathcote's Tally Ho were made at the booking office which stood outside the old Royal Hotel in High Street (where the Piazza Restaurant is today). Passengers on the Tally Ho could look forward to a great adventure from start to finish.

Departing from the pick-up point on the promenade the driver would announce his departure with a loud blast from his long brass post-horn and with a coach load of cheerful passengers the Tally Ho would make its journey along the promenade, swerve into the High Street and head for its destinations of Dyserth Waterfalls, Rhuddlan Castle, Bodelwyddan's Marble Church and Llanfairtalhaearn, then known as the "Little Switzerland of Wales".

The roads in those days were in a pitiful state - unmade, full of potholes, large stones and very dusty in the summer. It must be remembered that this type of early conveyance was unsprung with solid wooden wheels covered with a steel rim. Passengers sat on uncushioned wooden seats, at times very uncomfortable especially when the coach crossed over a hole or large stone.

On the move the heavy cumbersome coach at speed would sway from side to side resulting in many passengers suffering travel sickness. One woman living locally and now in her nineties has vivid memories of travelling in one of theses coaches as a youngster.

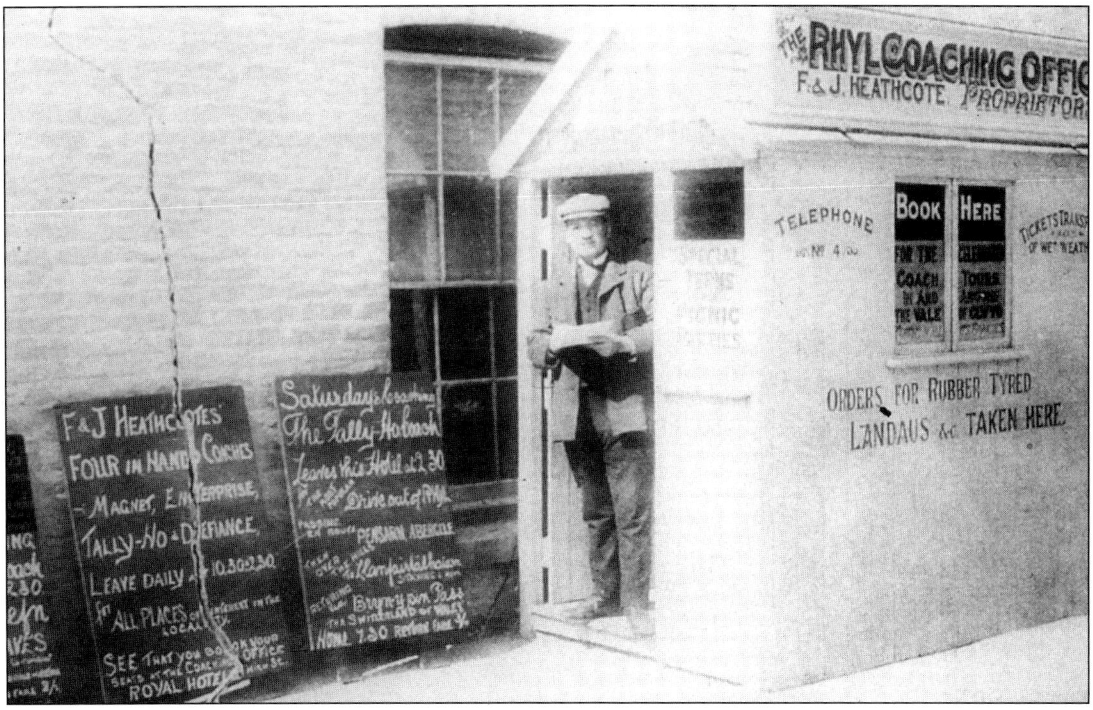

She relates her experience: "We had moments of intense excitement as the coach swayed from side to side, and our seats seemed dangerously high above the hedge tops. When the team of horses approached a hill or bend the slipping of horses hooves and the screeching of brakes made us hold our breath. It was also thrilling along the country roads which were often not wide enough for one vehicle to pass another. Also, pullovers, scarves and trews would have been more suitable than the long skirts and large hats we wore in those days, we were not emancipated then".

Nevertheless, the coach tour with all its faults provided an enjoyable, thrilling and memorable day for those who came to Rhyl for their seasonal holidays in those early days.
By 1912 Brookes Brothers White Rose Motors had replaced horse drawn vehicles for taking seaside visitors to the local beauty spots, no doubt in more comfort.

Above The Tally Ho's booking office pictured here in 1900. It stood near to the old Royal Hotel (where Piazza restaurant is today). A return fare tour to the local attractions was three shillings (15p).

Previous Page: The Tally Ho standing on Rhyl's promenade preparing to ferry passengers for a thrilling journey visiting local attractions.

Recalling Prestatyn's Much-Loved Silver Screen

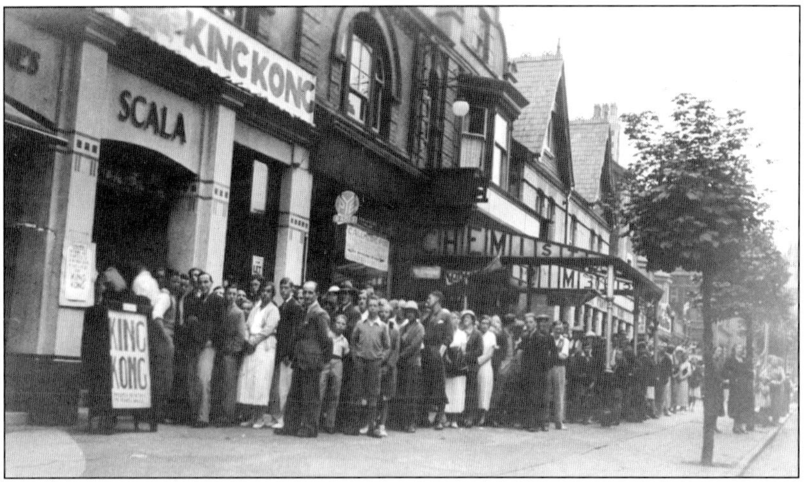

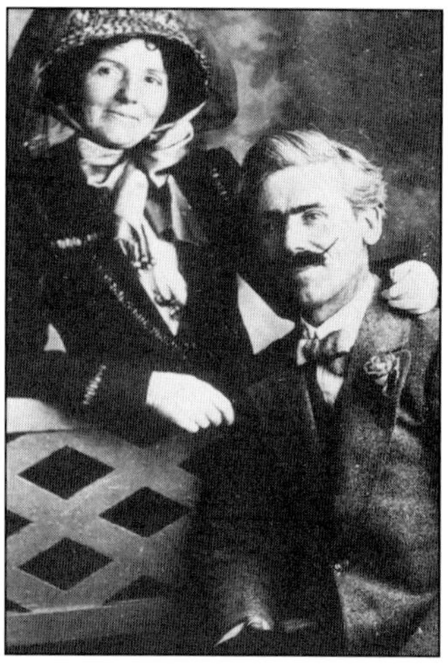

The oldest one-screened cinema in North Wales, Prestatyn's Scala Cinema closed its once welcoming doors for the last time in 1999 accompanying an end to a community's romantic attachment with what was a highly popular, well used, well attended and much loved family cinema, plundering from the community and its future generations a rich and irreplaceable part of Prestatyn's heritage and history a valuable and important asset to its future.

The older cinema-goers among us who visited the Scala in the early days will remember with affection when uniformed staff, a well dressed dickey-bowed manager and a bevvy of usherettes greeted an elated public to a world of escapism from the then often dull and drab routine of the real world and into the glitter, glamour and fantasy world of the silver screen. In the days when going to the cinema was a great adventure.

A regular to the Saturday matinees at the Scala as a teenager during the 1940's was John Parry of Gronant when they were showing films of Flash Gordon and Laurel and Hardy and when the Saturday matinee and a bag of chips after would amount to sixpence (3p). On his way home John would take off his shoes and roll up his trousers to collect duck eggs from Prestatyn's duck pond. He told me that his mother made *"cakes to die for"* with them, fond memories of happy days!

The first manager of the Scala was "Saronie". Born in Liverpool in 1872 his real name was James Roberts but he changed it to Saronie as it sounded more imposing in the world of cinematography. He started his career in Birkenhead where he was thought of as a pioneer of something that was almost magic. He once recalled that audiences were so astounded at the sight of a train rushing at them from the screen that they all jumped from their seats and ran to the back of the building.

Saronie was married to South Walian photographer Jane and they lived at "Hillcourt", Mount Ida Road, Prestatyn. By 1910 Saronie was showing films at Prestatyn's Town Hall for what was advertised as an "Exhibition of animated pictures" including the funeral of the late King.

In 1913 Saronie took over the Town Hall semi-permanently turning it into a cinema, later naming it as the Scala. During the 1930's the Scala was modernised with the removal of the old stage and screen, the roof raised to double the height and width and seating installed for 400 people.

The monster movie *"King Kong"* had its North Wales premier at the Scala in 1933 (pictured above left) with queues extending halfway up the High Street. A colourful character, Saronie would always greet the queues with a friendly chat and handshake. On seeing an attractive female on her own he would hold her hand and whisper to her "come with me my dear, I have a seat for you."

Saronie ended his career in 1963 and died aged 98 of a stroke in 1967. He is buried with his wife at Meliden: they had no children. They may have closed the doors of the Scala Cinema but the doors to our memories of the Scala will always be open.

Mixed Grills on Order for Stan and Ollie...

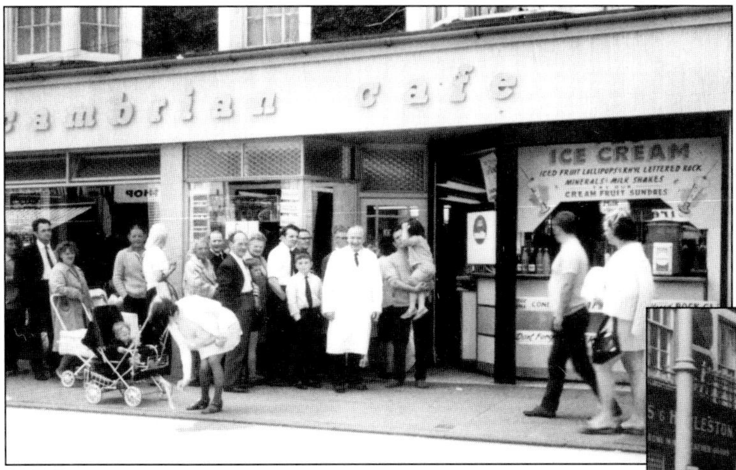

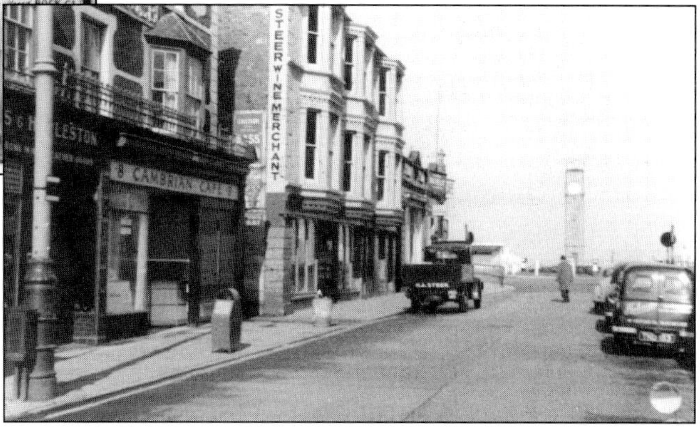

I was invited to visit Phillip Smith at his home in Prestatyn who told me how much he relished my Memory Lane page recalling Rhyl's old cafes and he went on to tell me in great detail that his father Lawrence Smith owned the Cambrian Café in Rhyl High Street (opposite to where "Cash Converters" is today).

Phillip very kindly opened up his overflowing family album for me to look through, and while I was savouring some superb photographs of the Cambrian and its staff, Phillip told me that his father opened the café in 1940 with a staff of over 30 (including 17 waitresses) and it soon became one of the most popular cafes in Rhyl. In those days the waitresses all wore black and white uniforms, white caps and white cuffs.

Phillip went on to say that there was always a permanent queue outside the Cambrian and he also remembered that most of the famous stars of the day who appeared at the Pavilion, Queens Theatre and Amphitheatre always came for lunch at the Cambrian.

Laurel and Hardy who appeared at the Queens in 1952 came for a meal and Phillip remembers them both tucking into a large mixed grill each. Other stars of the day Phillip remembers calling in were comedians Tommy Trinder and Jimmy Clitheroe and bandleader Victor Sylvester. Noelle Gordon of Crossroads fame also visited the café whenever she was in Rhyl and Phillip told me she became a good friend of the family who went on holiday cruises with them many times.

Although the Cambrian closed in 1984 Phillip has many happy and fond memories of one of the most popular and well-loved cafes in Rhyl and they are forever glued in the album of his memories. After being shown the photographs of the Cambrian and very kindly being given a plateful of ham rolls, biscuits and cakes by Phillips wife Ruth, I left the very friendly hospitable couple's house feeling had I ever had the opportunity to have enjoyed a meal at the Cambrian I am sure the hospitality would have been just as warm and friendly.

Bottom: The High Street photograph of the Cambrian is dated 1958.

Top: The front view photo showing owner Lawrence Smith in his white coat, was taken in 1978.

A Town Steeped in History and Heritage

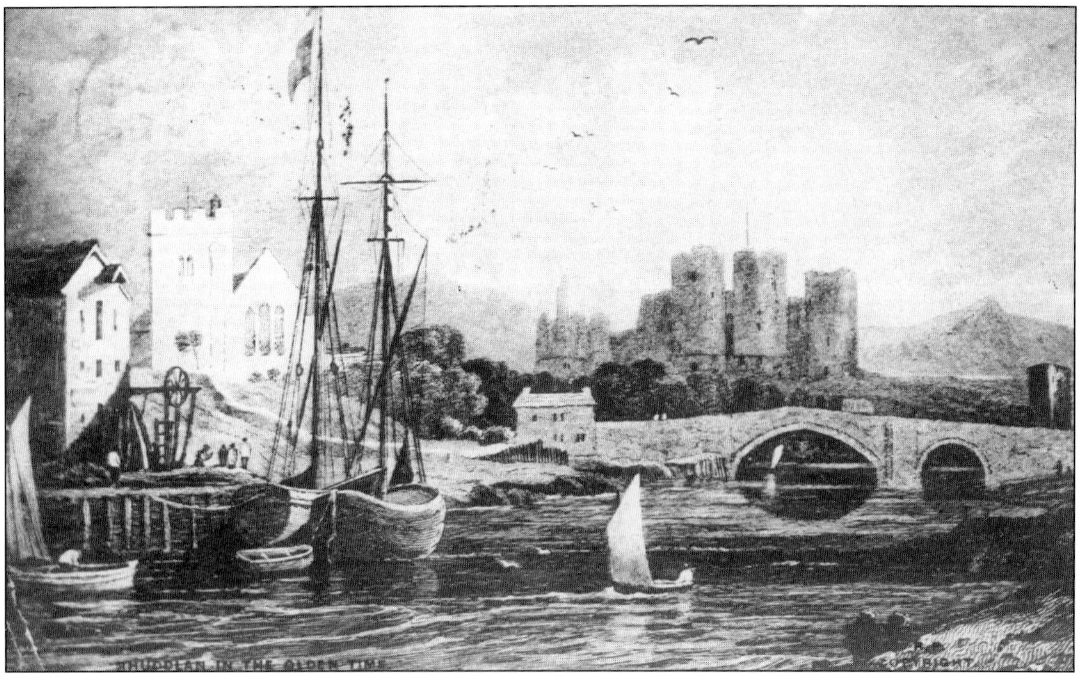

Steeped in history, the illustrious ancient town of Rhuddlan with its once industrious port and famous castle also has an impressive association with several Princes, a Norman Marquis and an English King and Queen. There can be few towns in Wales that can boast such a unique heritage.

Rhuddlan is recorded in the Doomsday book of 1086 as Roeland, its name changed many times through the centuries from Rothelan to Rudlan and Ruthlan. The present days spelling appeared around 1577, even then it was not officially used until 1896 when the local council gave the name its approval.

When King Edward I built Rhuddlan Castle he found it essential for the security and the shipping of goods to the castle to provide a deep water channel from the castle to the sea. It imposed a major engineering problem for the king and his men. Using the most primitive tools it eventually took 77 men working six days a week three years from 1277 to 1280 to complete, which is the present day River Clwyd.

During the 18th and 19th centuries Rhuddlan had an important and industrious port, with its harbour, wharves and warehouses. Ships sailed regularly from Rhuddlan to Liverpool, Dublin and other ports with goods of every description, which included grain, salt, timber and lead ore from the Talargoch lead mines.

Until the opening of the Vale of Clwyd Railway in 1858 Rhuddlan remained the main port for the Vale. Goods unloaded from moored ships alongside Rhuddlan Quay, were carried in large wheeled vehicles throughout Rhuddlan and district.

The ruined castle, a legacy from Rhuddlan's colourful past was built over a period of five years from 1277 by Edward I. Previously there had been two fortresses on the site of the castle one built in 1015 by Prince Llewelyn ap Seisyllt, the other built in 1073 by Robert of Rhuddlan, a Norman Marquess and cousin of Richard II , this consisted of a tower and courtyard only. Edward I was to spend three Christmas festivals at Rhuddlan and Queen Eleanor gave birth at the castle to Princess Elizabeth. In the 13th century coal was carried to the castle from the coal pits at Mostyn.

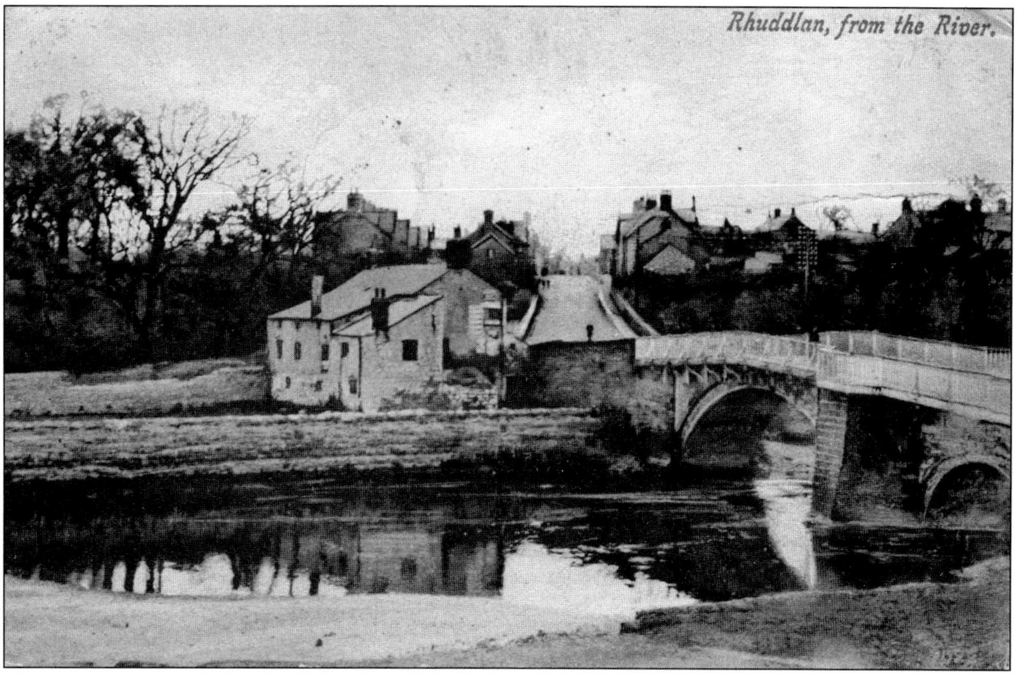

The present condition of the town's castle is the result of the damage it suffered at the hands of the Parliamentary Army in 1646. The bridge over the River Clwyd was originally made of wood, constructed in such a way that it could be lifted or swung aside for the passage of shipping. The bridge was damaged in the war between Llewelyn ap Gruffudd and Edward I in 1277.

In 1358 the bridge this time was built as a solid stone bridge to be restyled by the Bishop William Hughes of St Asaph in 1595. Other notes of historic interest is that Rhuddlan at one time had its own mint where silver coins were produced in the reign of William the Conqueror, 1066-87 and Henry II, 1216-72.

There were 11 public houses in Rhuddlan at one time, three of them had nautical connections. They were the Ship, the Anchor and the Mariners Arms, (corner of High Street and Church street). The National Eisteddfod was also held at Rhuddlan Castle in 1850.

When you are next passing through Rhuddlan take time to notice and discover an ancient, colourful town steeped in history and relics of a bygone age.

Above: Rhuddlan Bridge seen on this 1910 postcard was originally made of wood, constructed in such a way so that it could be lifted or swung aside for the passing of ships.

Previous Page: Rhuddlan's unique heritage and history is embodied in this 1830 print.

A Peach by the Beach.

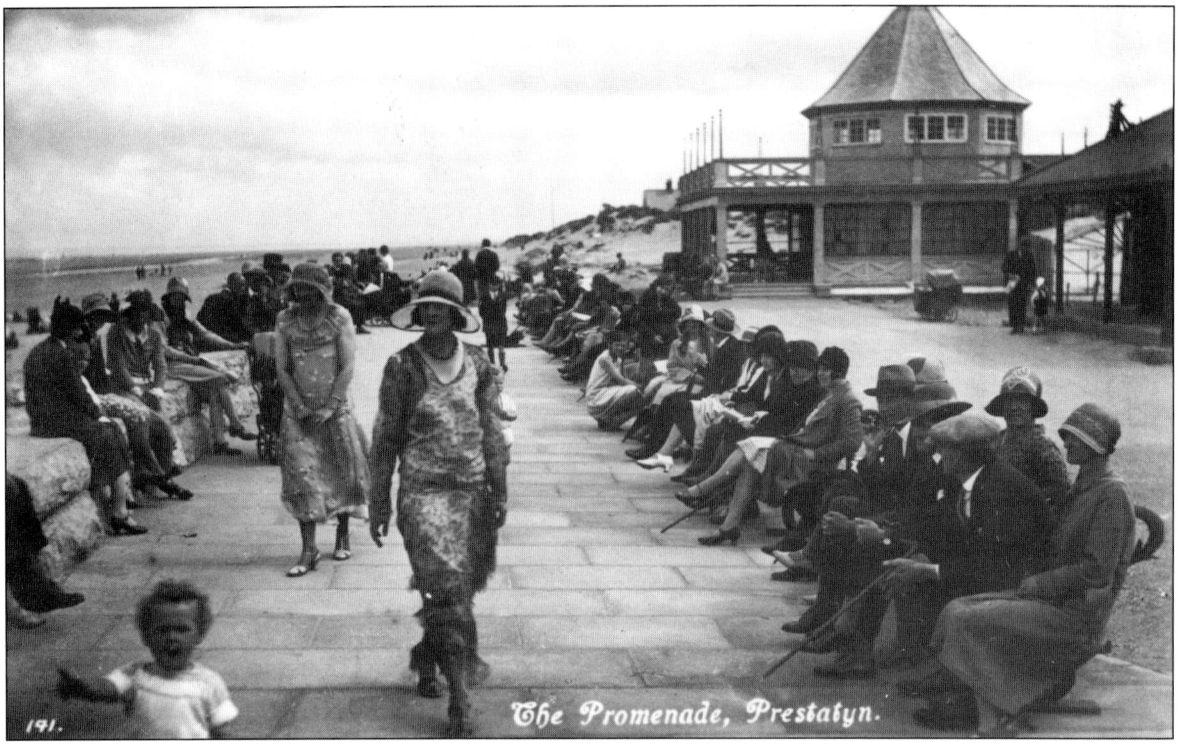

The reasons are not hard to find as to why Prestatyn, the oldest resort town in North Wales, became a favourite destination for thousands of eager 20th century holiday makers and day trippers during those less-hurried, never-ending, blazing summer days of long ago.

The popularity, prosperity and growth of Prestatyn started with the opening of the town's railway station in 1848, when the population of Prestatyn was only 500 (today the estimated population is 18,496 according to the 2001 census).

Vast numbers came to Prestatyn in those early years from the smoke and noise-filled towns and cities to savour the delights of the sun, sea, sand and the pure air that Prestatyn had to offer (as it still does today).

Many of these visitors suffered from chest and bronchial complaints, brought on from the smoky industrial areas they lived in in those days, coming to Prestatyn on the advice of their doctors who told them that the ozone-filled seaside air would cure their complaints, and for many it did.

Prestatyn's first guide book was published in 1913 and makes for enlightening reading that captures the spirit of the age. It declares that: "Owing to its sheltered position from the east winds and its open front to the Irish Sea, the air is always highly charged and holds in minute particles of sea water ozone, this renders the climate particularly suitable to invalids suffering from diseases of air passages, and it's well known that many of Prestatyn's residents came here in a critical state of health.

"For the delicate children and patients suffering from a nervous breakdown, Prestatyn is eminently adopted during any month. The loveliest resort in Wales owes its charm and popularity to its picturesque setting between hills and sea and partly to its sea air like wine and honey.

The exceptionally good ultra violet content of the sunshine is due to complete absence of smog and smoke, combine to form an ideal holiday atmosphere. Children of all ages find it a paradise, sand-castle building, donkeys and the pierrots all are here for their diversion."

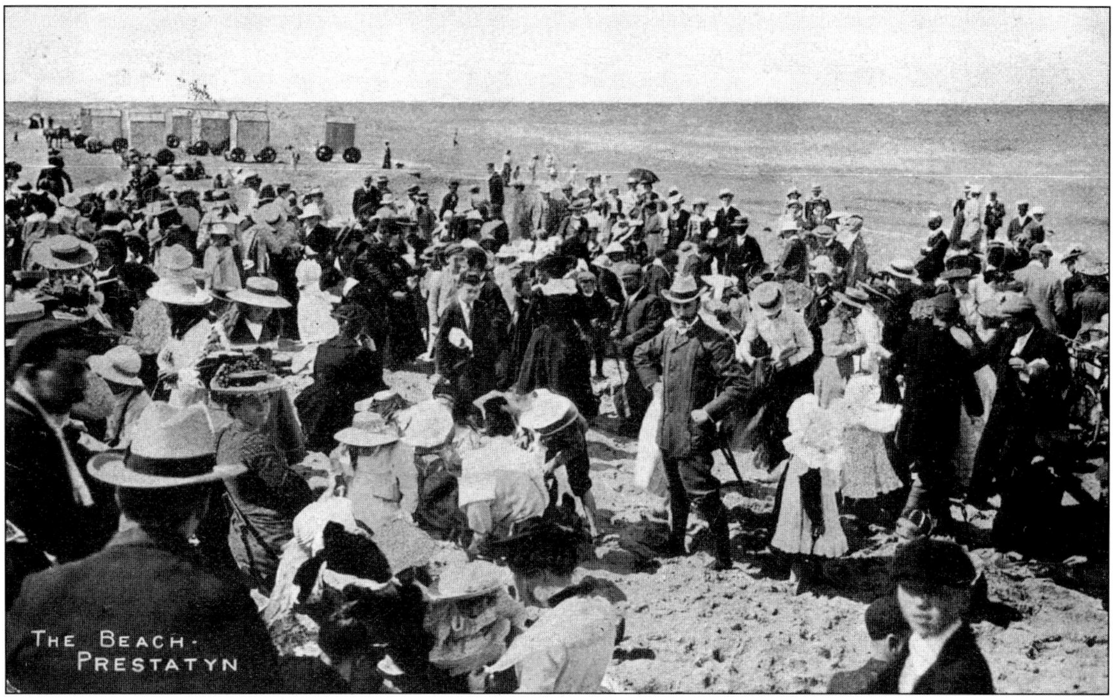

Some years ago a visitor paid a casual visit to Prestatyn, he was the victim of a severe bronchial complaint. Coming to a sudden standstill opposite Penisardre (where the precinct is today) and glancing up at the evergreen oaks he remarked to his companions: "Well if evergreen oak flourishes so well in this neighbourhood, it is just the climate I need."

Thereupon he decided to stay several weeks with the result that his complaint disappeared.

Arriving in Prestatyn, these early holiday makers lodged at many of the boarding houses in the town. The favoured ones being Park House in Nant Hall Road, the Edgemond and Hawarden House in Victoria Road and Summerfield and Bastion Houses in Bastion Road.

The beach or taking a seat or a walk along the prom would be favourite attractions.

"So if you are ill, don't take a pill, I'll tell you something better still, for sunshine and air, weather that's fair and health-giving rest, Prestatyn is best."

Above: This card shows a crowd scene on Prestatyn beach in 1908, the beachwear is quaintly outdated, don't you think? They certainly did have hot summers in those days, notice the man in his suit and trilby!

Previous Page: This card is a superb slice of seaside social history from the 1920's, it flaunts the fashion in the clothes of the day as this elegant lady demonstrates on her own "cat- walk" on Prestatyn promenade, the building in the background was the very popular Beach Café.

The Indispensable Corner Shop

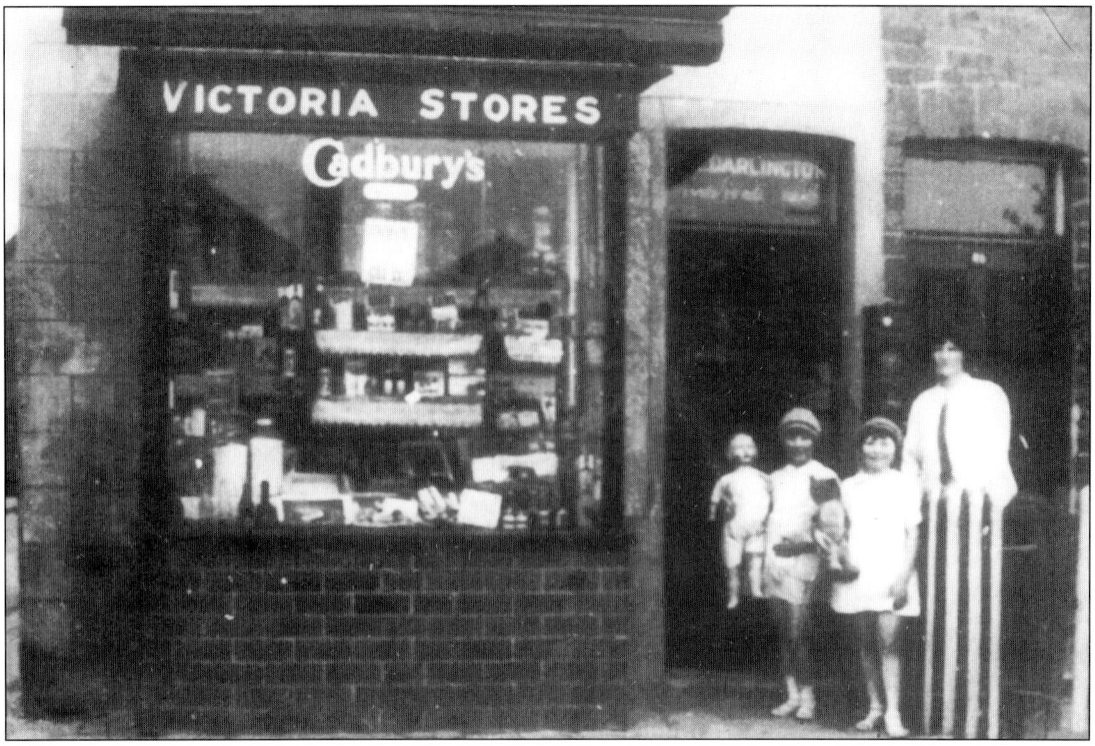

Victoria Stores, Victoria Road, Rhyl, pictured above in the 1940's was one of the many indispensable "corner" type shops that flourished in the town, where personal service with a smile and a few minutes of local gossip were commonplace to those most important of people, the customer. Qualities that are essential when shopping and sadly missing from the hurried and impersonal environment of today's supermarket store.

Pictured outside Victoria Stores are the owner Mrs Elizabeth Darlington and her daughters Phyllis and Doris. The popularity of Victoria Stores and the friendliness of Mrs Darlington became so recognised that the shop became fondly known as "Aunty Darli's".

Mrs Darlington supplied everything a corner shop sold in those days, and everything for the customer's daily needs, from bread, bacon, cheese, butter and eggs to confectionery and cigarettes. Selling two cigarettes and two matches to those customers who didn't have enough money to buy a full packet.

Today the old Victoria Stores is occupied by Sargents the vet. The old advertising such as Cadbury's, Fry's chocolate, Colman's Starch and Mustard, and Hudson's Soap embellished every shop window in addition to the enamel advertising on the walls of every shop corner, and in those days a product could be advertised with certainty of some permanence.

In these days we fall easily into nostalgic mood, it seems we enjoy embracing and thinking more about the past than we do about the present or future.

Nothing recalls the so-called 'good old days' quite so vividly as an advertising slogan, the advertiser's name still stirs the memories of our parents' and grandparents generations.

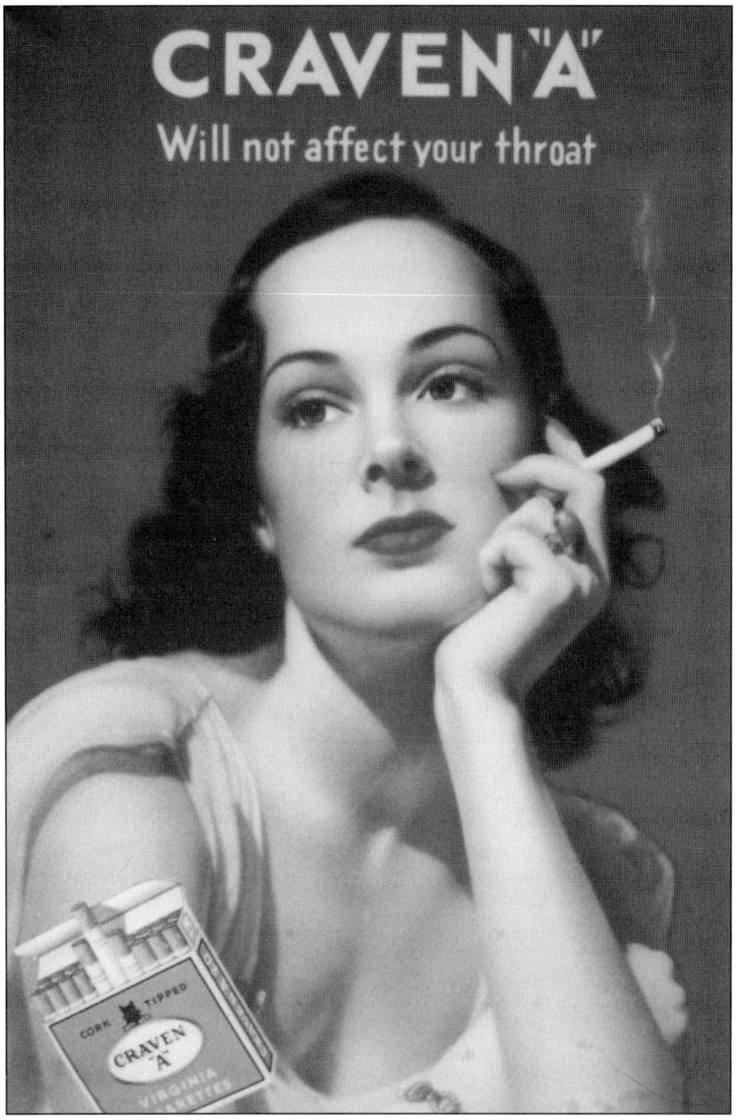

Who could ever forget those advertising slogans that became as permanent as the enamel signs they were printed on.

Claims such as :

Craven "A" will not affect your throat.
Player's please. A packet in every pocket.
Beecham's Pills. Worth a guinea a box.
Pears Soap. Matchless for the complexion.
Oxo. Beef in brief.
Woodbine. The great little cigarette.
Veno's lightening cough cure. Cures colds, and chest diseases.
Tizer. The appetiser.
Bovril. Prevents that sinking feeling.
Ogdens St Bruno. The tobacco that won't be hurried.
Fry's chocolate. By Royal Appointment.

This advert in rhyme for Beecham's Pills was at one time placed in the newspapers at Christmas: "Hark the herald angels sing, Beecham's Pills are just the thing, peace on earth and mercy mild, two for an adult and one for a child".

Also this pleasant little rhyme for Pendleton's ice cream which dates from the 1960s hits the right button: "There was a girl from Southend, who only had tuppence to spend, what could be nicer than a Pendletons Twicer, an ice-cream with a lolly each end".

Previous Page: The corner Store: Victoria Stores in Victoria Road, Rhyl 1940s.

Above: Craven A. A popular old cigarette advert from the 1940s.

Prestatyn Railway's Golden Age

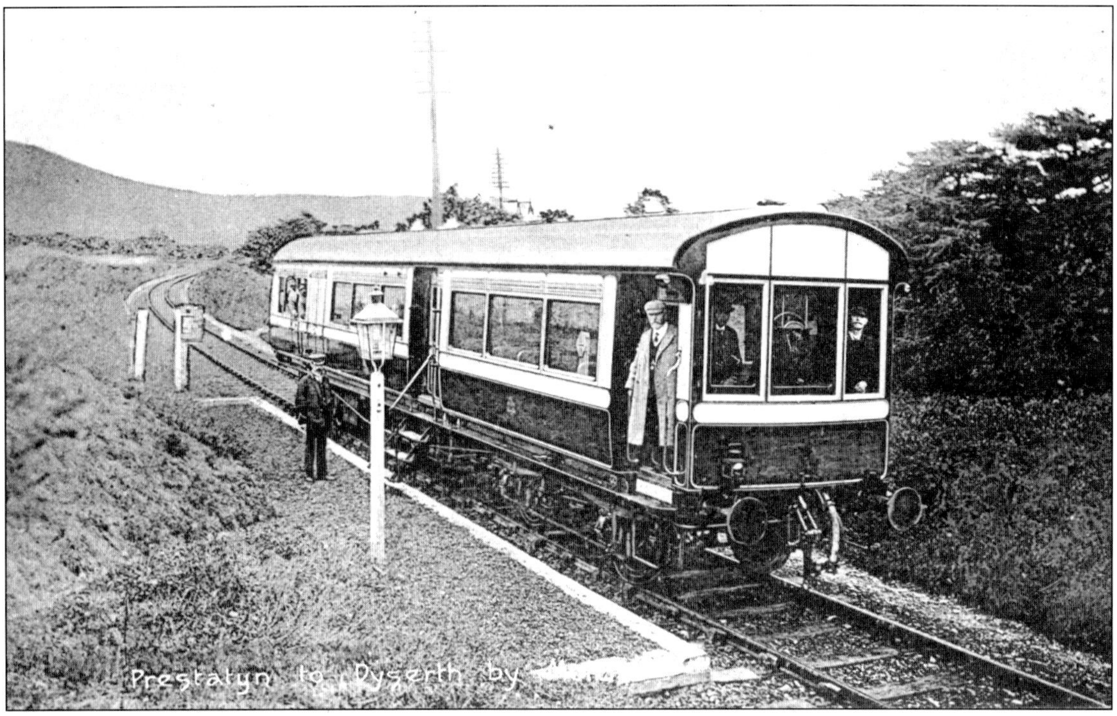

A great love affair and a brief encounter with a local train service proved so favourable with passengers on the Prestatyn to Dyserth Railway in early 1906 that on August Bank Holiday Monday it attracted a record 2,000+ passengers resulting in a crowded train on nearly every journey. On one occasion forty people were left behind at Meliden. Many visitors were also travelling on the Railmotor as it was known simply for enjoyment and pleasure.

The line was opened due to the increasing population and popularity of Prestatyn and Dyserth as tourist attractions and the demand for transport between the neighbourhoods by more rapid and convenient means than by walking or horse drawn vehicles.

It eventually took 150 men three years to lay the two and three quarter mile track from Prestatyn to Dyserth, at a vast cost in those days of £29,978. The line was finally opened on August 26, 1905, in front of a large crowd on Prestatyn station and a host of local councillors, railway officials, local MPs and invited guests.

The opening was performed by John and Phylis Ree, children of the chief goods manager of the line Frank Ree. John blew the whistle while Phyllis waved the green flag.

The steam driven Railmotor had two compartments each capable of accommodating 24 passengers. Folding steps were used where there was no platform. Drivers, Dan Jones and Walter Fowles both from Rhyl were the Railmotor's regular crew until they both retired in 1928.

Commencing from Prestatyn station the halts along the line were Chapel Street (at the end of Maes -y-Groes), Rhuddlan Road, (renamed Woodland Park in 1923), Meliden and Dyserth, the fare to Dyserth was three- pence (1½p)

Travelling at an average speed of 25mph the journey to Dyserth would take fifteen minutes and on an average day the railmotor carried between four to five hundred passengers, with up to fourteen journeys during the summer months.

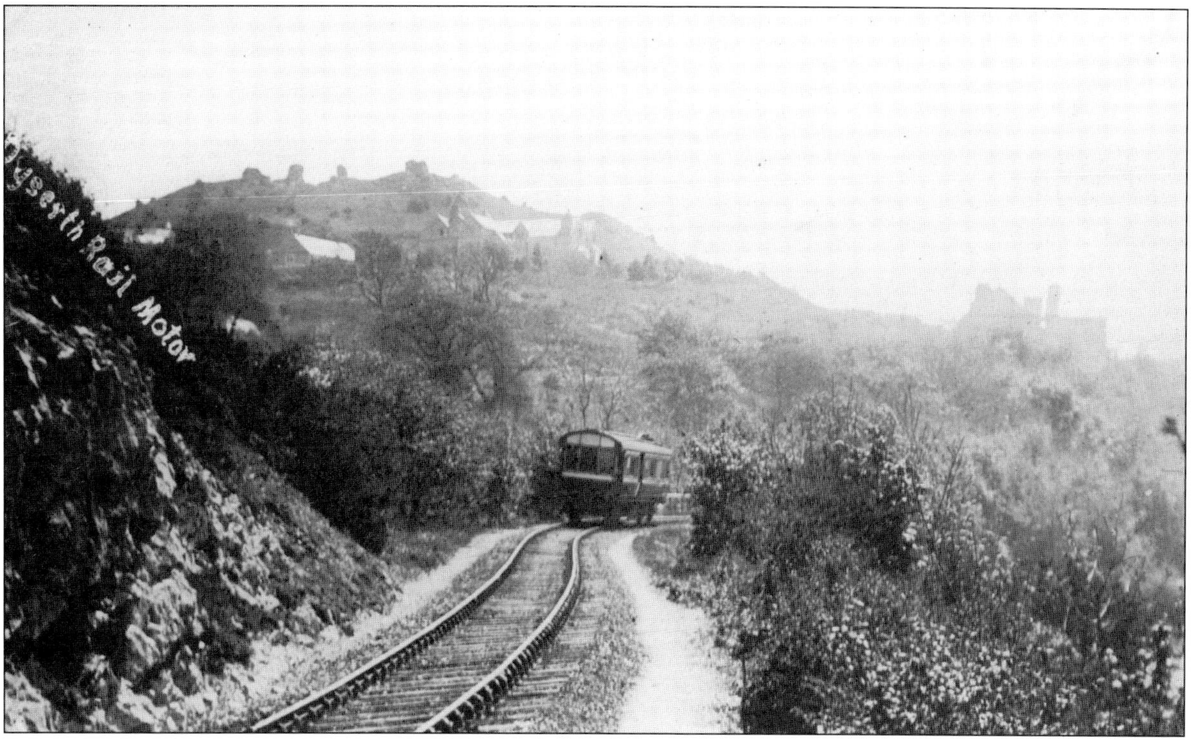

An early guide book to Prestatyn describes the delightful and captivating journey - "The Railmotor starts at the main line station and after calling two way side stops, skirts the hills with an ever varying panorama of woodland scenery on one hand, with the broad green plain stretching seawards on the other. Passing Meliden, the Railmotor pursues its way through many curves through a pretty wood showing glimpses of Rhyl and the Vale of Clwyd with Moel Hirraddug in the background".

During the lazy summer months, visitors would take the opportunity to walk from Dyserth to Marian Mills where afternoon tea and home made buttered scones would be served. The demise of the Railmotor came with the introduction of the cheaper and more convenient Crosville bus service in 1930.

The last Railmotor ran to Dyserth on September 20, 1930. Had the tracks to the line survived rather than being ripped out, and a smaller-gauge passenger train introduced, it would undoubtedly have become Prestatyn's greatest attraction.

Above: The scenic route of the Prestatyn to Dyserth railways is vividly captured on this 1913 postcard as it skirts through wooded hillside on its journey from Dyserth to Meliden. Note the ruins of Dyserth Castle on top of the hill in the background built by Henry III in 1241 and razed to the ground in 1263.

Previous Page: Time for a "photo-call" as the Railmotor pauses for a picture at Rhuddlan Road halt in 1905.

Below: Ladies from the Volunteer Aid Detachment (V.A.D.) Dyserth Station 1914-1918

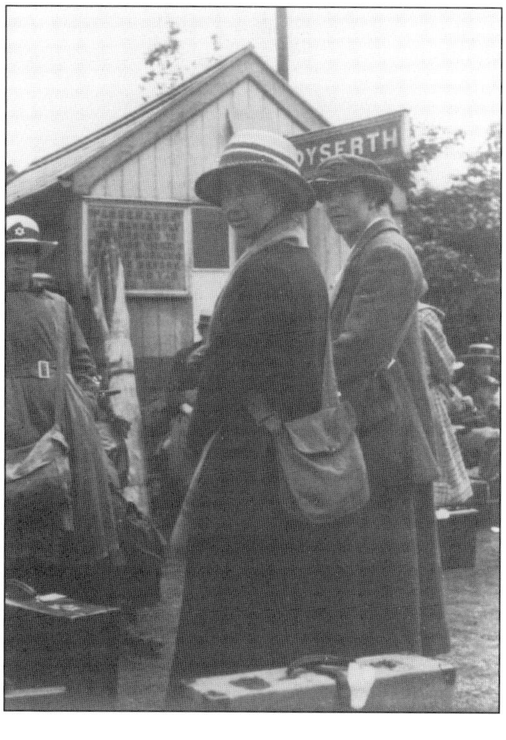

Wartime Pints and Pilots

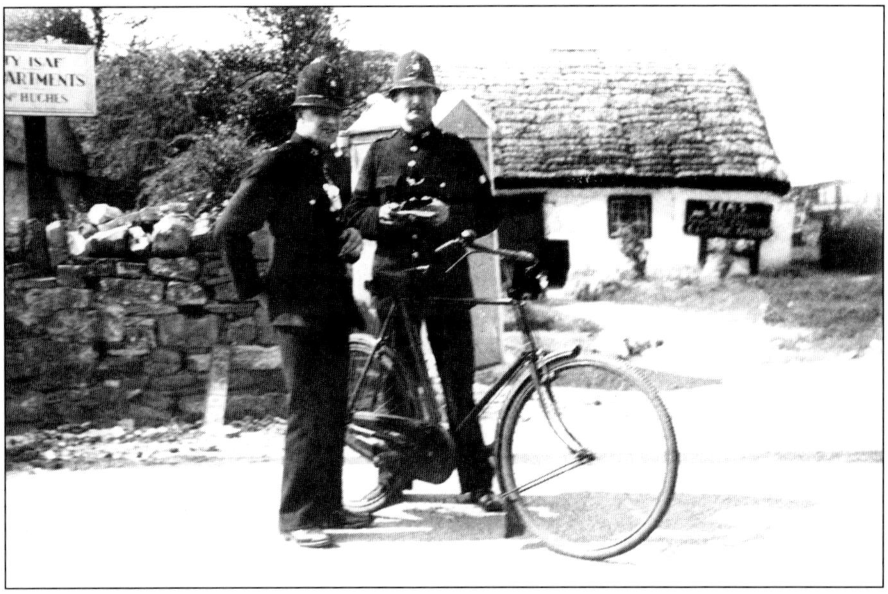

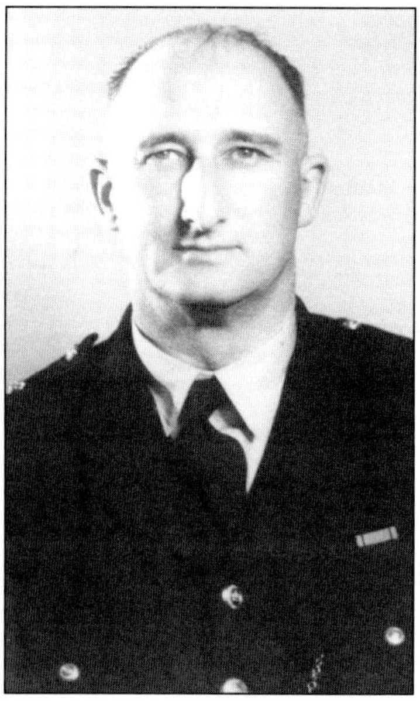

The original name for the Farmers Arms pub in the village of Ffynnongroyw was the Farmers Tavern, it changed its name in the early 1900s to the Farmers Inn, eventually arriving at its present day name. An early edition of Sutton's Trade Directory notes that by 1889, the Farmers Tavern had joined Railway Tavern and the Crown as the three public houses in the village (as they still are today).

Ffynnongroyw's All Saints Parish Church, which celebrated its centenary in 1983, originally started in a room at the rear of the Farmers and it's safe to say that alcohol didn't appear on the list of refreshments at their meetings!

The landlords of the Farmers between 1924 and 1943 were Thomas and Mary Williams who, at the time, had their 11-year old grandson Jerry Vernon living with them, and it was his keen observations and actions that implicated him in saving the life of a spitfire pilot during the Second World War.

The dark days of the 1940s were a time when there were German raids on parts of Liverpool and the waters of the River Dee were busy with the movement of heavy shipping traffic, but through all this upheaval the traditional British pint could still be had in the peaceful surroundings of the Farmers Arms pub.

During the times Thomas and Mary Williams were serving in the bar at the Farmers, their grandson remained in the living room indulging in his favourite hobby of observing through binoculars for hours on end, the movements of the coal-carrying boats at Point of Ayr Colliery and the iron-ore boats at Mostyn Docks.

It was during those observations that Jerry saw a cloud of smoke three miles west of Hilbre Island off the Wirral. He also noticed to his surprise, a parachute below the volume of smoke. He rushed into the bar to inform his grandfather, and although he possessed a telephone, he didn't know which service to call, he therefore sent his grandson to report the incident to the village policeman, Archie Roberts, who lived in a house around the corner in Mornant Avenue (the village didn't have a police station at that time.)

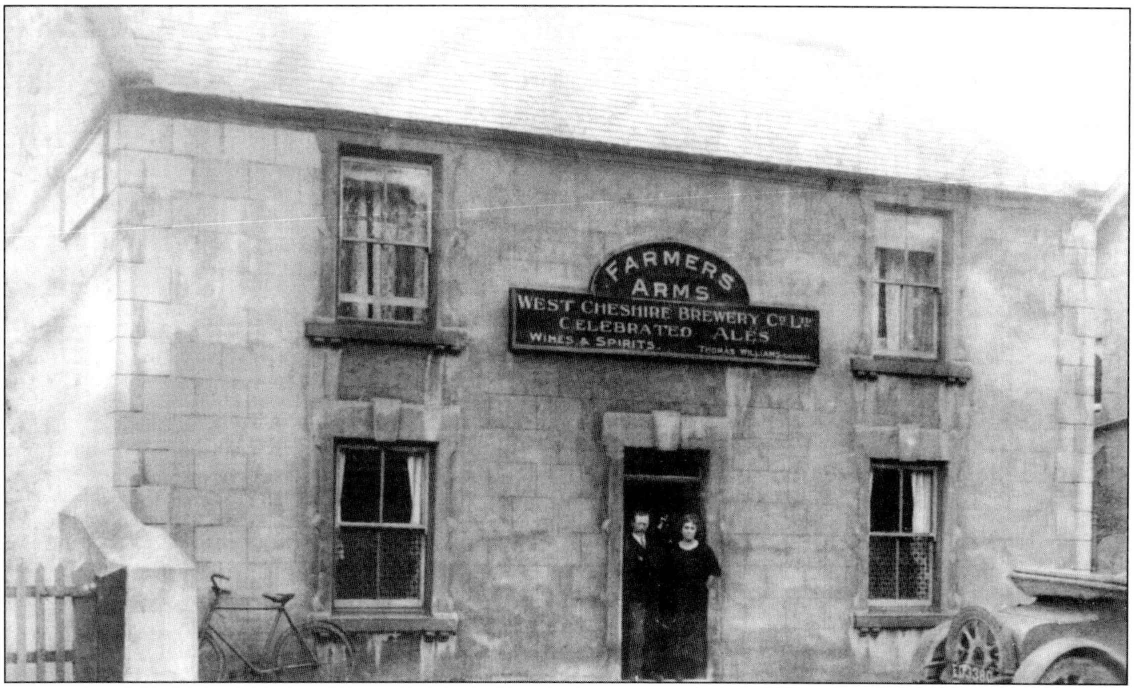

Archie Roberts disliked anyone wandering around the village at night and would lurk in shop doorways waiting to chase home any unsuspecting youngster.

When Jerry arrived at Archie's house and told him of the parachute incident, he was questioned as to whether he was 'story-telling' instructing him to go home as he would attend to it.

Archie informed the Air Ministry and a rescue boat was sent out. PC Archie Roberts and Thomas and Mary Williams were later told the airman was successfully rescued after bailing out of his Spitfire. Afterwards they all received letters of commendation, but the real hero in this intriguing story is the grandson, Jerry Vernon, don't you think?

During the war two bombs fell on Ffynnongroyw, one landed in a field alongside the Crown Hotel, the other fell between Llinegr Farm and the hill, the only casualty was a cow that died when shrapnel entered its stomach.

Today the grandson Jerry Vernon is 75 years old and lives in Prestatyn. I am grateful to him for allowing us to share some of his cherished memories.

Previous Page Left Photo: PC Archie Roberts (right) and Prestatyn policeman Ednyfed Davies pictured at Gronant crossroads in the 1940s, the cottage in the background (long since demolished) is where Pen Isaf bungalow is today.

Previous Page Right Photo: PC Archie Roberts

Above: Landlords Thomas and Mary Williams in the doorway to the Farmers Arms, Ffynnongroyw, in 1924

Lighthouse Monument to the Lives Saved at Sea

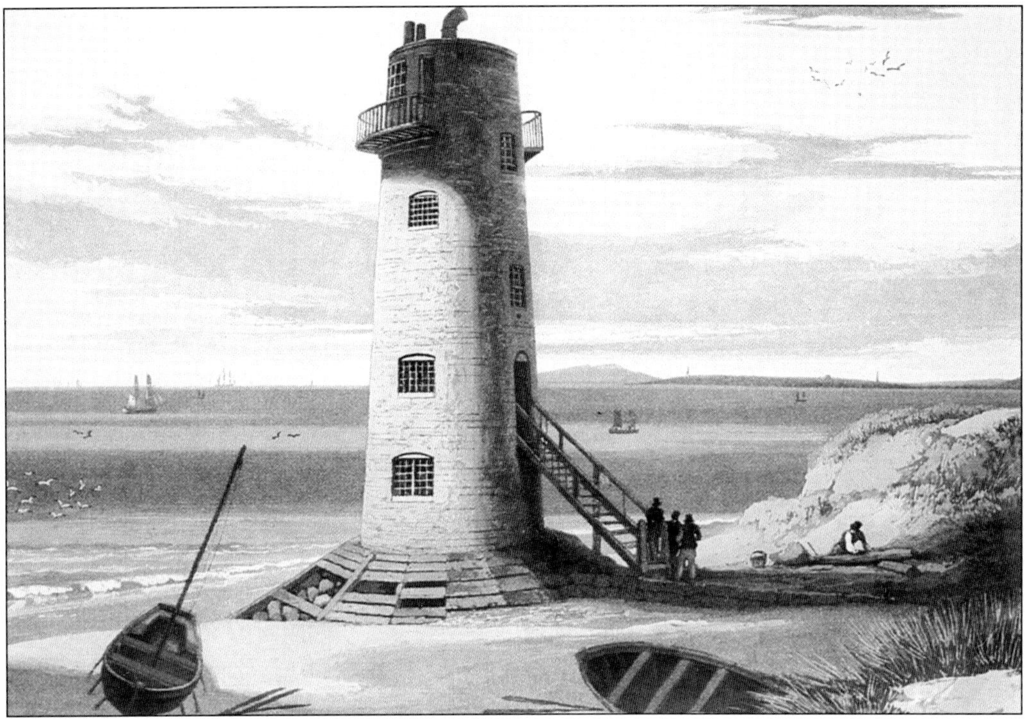

The tallest and most notable land-mark along the North Wales coast is the Point of Ayr lighthouse at Talacre. The first welcoming light across the waters of the Dee Estuary shone out on September 30th, 1777, and continued to guide a thriving shipping trade in and out of the Irish Sea to the port of Mostyn, the docks at Greenfield, Bagillt and Flint, the steelworks at Shotton and the flourishing shipbuilding yards at Queensferry and Sandycroft.

There had been disastrous losses on the outer estuary bank, including a double tragedy in 1775. Two boats the Trevor and Non Pareil, which were heading for Dublin, were swept onto sand banks resulting in the loss of 200 passengers and crew, and cargoes of precious stones, silks, spices and woollens worth thousands of pounds.

The bodies from the boats were swept onto the beaches of Gronant and Talacre where they were robbed and stripped of their valuables.

A month later a meeting held by the merchants of the ports of Chester decided that a light to the entrance of the Dee was urgently needed to show safe passage through the river's estuary.

Talacre's first brick-built lighthouse was built at a cost of just over £349 in 1777 and stood 52 feet high. The first lighthouse keeper was Edward Price who was paid 16 guineas (£16.80) a year. There were early difficulties as the oil lamps that lit the lighthouse light would smoke and cloud the light, and the oil would also freeze during the winter. Eventually the light came from special candles and a host of reflecting mirrors. This system was replaced in 1816 by an argand lamp, which was a scientifically constructed lamp that gave 10 times the light of earlier lamps as well as a cleaner flame.

This first lighthouse became badly damaged by years of pounding storms undermined and collapsed into the sea in 1818. The present 99ft stone-built lighthouse was built in 1819 to the designs of Robert Stevenson, a civil engineer specialising in lighthouse construction. The walls of the new lighthouse were painted with red and white bands, with a blinking light that had a range of 19 miles.

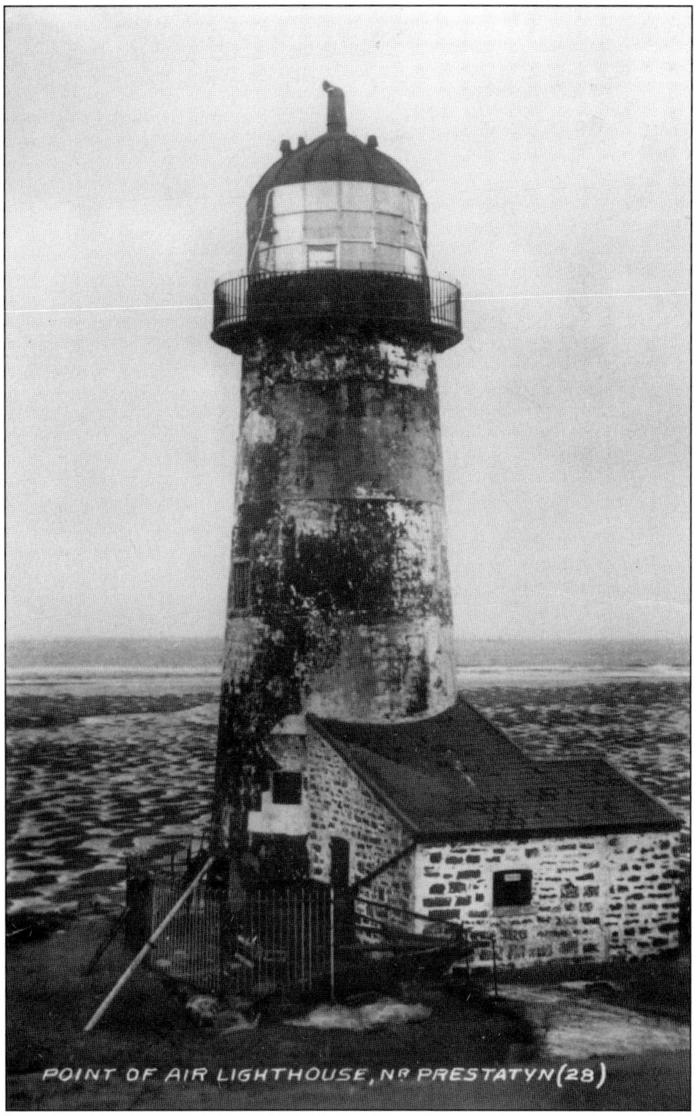

In 1958 the five-floored lighthouse was offered for sale at the local estate agents at £1,500. It was described as 'having an entrance hall with adjoining toilet and kitchen below; a living room and three bedrooms, one above the other - the top one being the old lantern house with a balcony around it'.

By 1988, the lighthouse had been cosily converted into a five-floored detached residence. Estate agents described it as ' one of the more out-of the-ordinary properties and a sound proposition for someone who wants to tell stories about life at sea. But one word of warning - quicksands make it almost impossible to be reached by car and the sea surrounds the place completely at high tide. At £15,000 it is a real bargain'.

Today the oldest lighthouse in Wales is the property of James McAllister of Talacre Beach Caravan Sales Ltd, who purchased it in 1983, and shipping traffic through the Dee is now guided by lighted buoys. Point of Ayr lighthouse is a valuable and important example of maritime heritage and stands as a stark reminder and a monument to the many lives it saved out at sea.

Previous Page: The first Point of Ayr Lighthouse at Talacre in 1815.

Above: Point of Ayr lighthouse in 1930

Rhyl's Mummy in the Cupboard

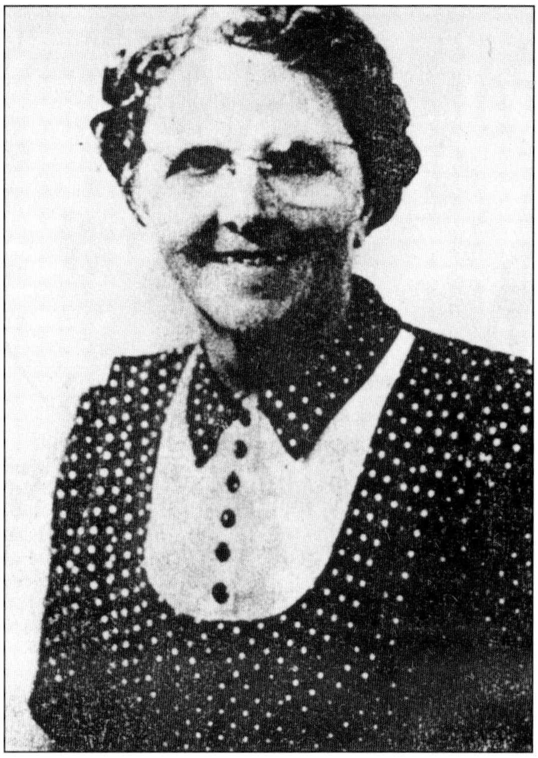

In April 1960 the small, pale-complexioned Sarah Jane Harvey, who lived at 35 West Kinmel Street, Rhyl, and resembled everyone's favourite grandmother, was admitted to Royal Alexandra Hospital in Rhyl for observations.

Her taxi driver son, Leslie, who had lived with his mother until 1955, had decided to give her a pleasant surprise, or so he thought, by taking advantage of her confinement to decorate the house for her. On the landing at the top of the stairs stood a cupboard which he remembered being told never to open, as it contained the belongings of former tenant, Frances Knight, who Leslie vaguely remembered. To decorate the landing, Leslie needed to open the cupboard backing onto the wall.

When he eventually forced the doors open with a knife, he saw what looked like a dust covered bundle inside. Obtaining a torch he shone the light inside and stood back in shock when he saw a foot sticking out of the 'bundle'. Leslie rushed to find his father-in-law and after further examination, informed the police of his gruesome discovery.

By late evening the usually quiet street was now bustling with police, two forensic scientists from Preston, a pathologist, biologist, and the coroner, Rhys Jones. Despite the hideous appearance of the face, Leslie Harvey observed that it bore some resemblance to former lodger Francis Knight. Mrs Knight, he recalled, had been a divorcee living on a small weekly maintenance from her former dentist husband, but he thought she had left in 1940.

The body they all looked at was in a doubled up position and clothed in a now faded night-dress, the skin was shrunken and leathery and the body had been mummified by the process of years of warm air circulating through the cupboard.

The discovery started a major police investigation in very mysterious circumstances. It was the task of the pathologist to undertake a difficult post mortem, and the mummified body was soaked in a glycerine solution for a week.

The pathologist in addition discovered a stocking ligature and a groove around the neck claiming it

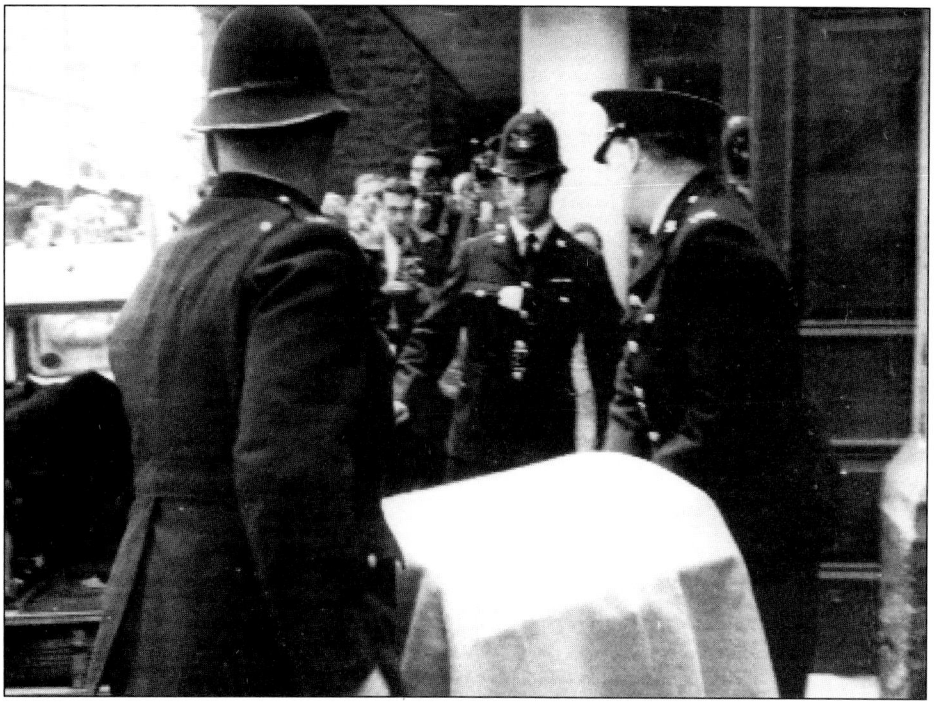

was consistent with strangulation, and through subsequent inquiries the police were treating the case as one of murder.

When Jane Harvey was discharged from hospital she was interviewed at Rhyl police station where, in her first statement to detectives, she said 'I don't understand the body being there, I don't know who it is!'

In a later statement to detectives she told them 'I will tell you what happened "Mrs Knight was my lodger and she was badly crippled, I heard screaming coming from her bedroom, I saw her on the floor, she was in terrible pain and I tried to put her back in bed, but I couldn't. I went to make her a cup of tea, and when I took it up to her she had died, so I pulled her along the landing and put her in the cupboard, put in some fly paper and locked it. 'I was so scared so I kept going to collect her two pounds a week maintenance" (over twenty years this had mounted up to £2,099).

Arrested for murder, Jane Harvey later appeared at Ruthin Assizes, where she pleaded not guilty to murder and guilty of intent to defraud.

The prosecution alleged that shortly after Mrs Harvey was given permission to draw Mrs Knight's money, she strangled her with a stocking, the defence maintained that the stocking was applied in life. In her defence, she told the court that 'Mrs Knight had been suffering from a bad cold and it's common knowledge to wrap a stocking around the neck for the cure of colds,' the court was said to have 'stirred in disbelief' at her implications.

The Crown could not prove that the knotted ligature had caused Frances Knights death, and there was no case of murder to answer, but she was found guilty of obtaining money by deception and sentenced to 15 months imprisonment. On her release she went to stay at an old people's home where she died of cancer.

The Rhyl 'mummy in the cupboard' story captured the interest of the world's media at the time and is possibly the town's most mysterious unsolved death.

Above: The mummified remains of Frances Knight being carried out of the house in West Kinmel Street.

Previous Page: Sarah Jane Harvey